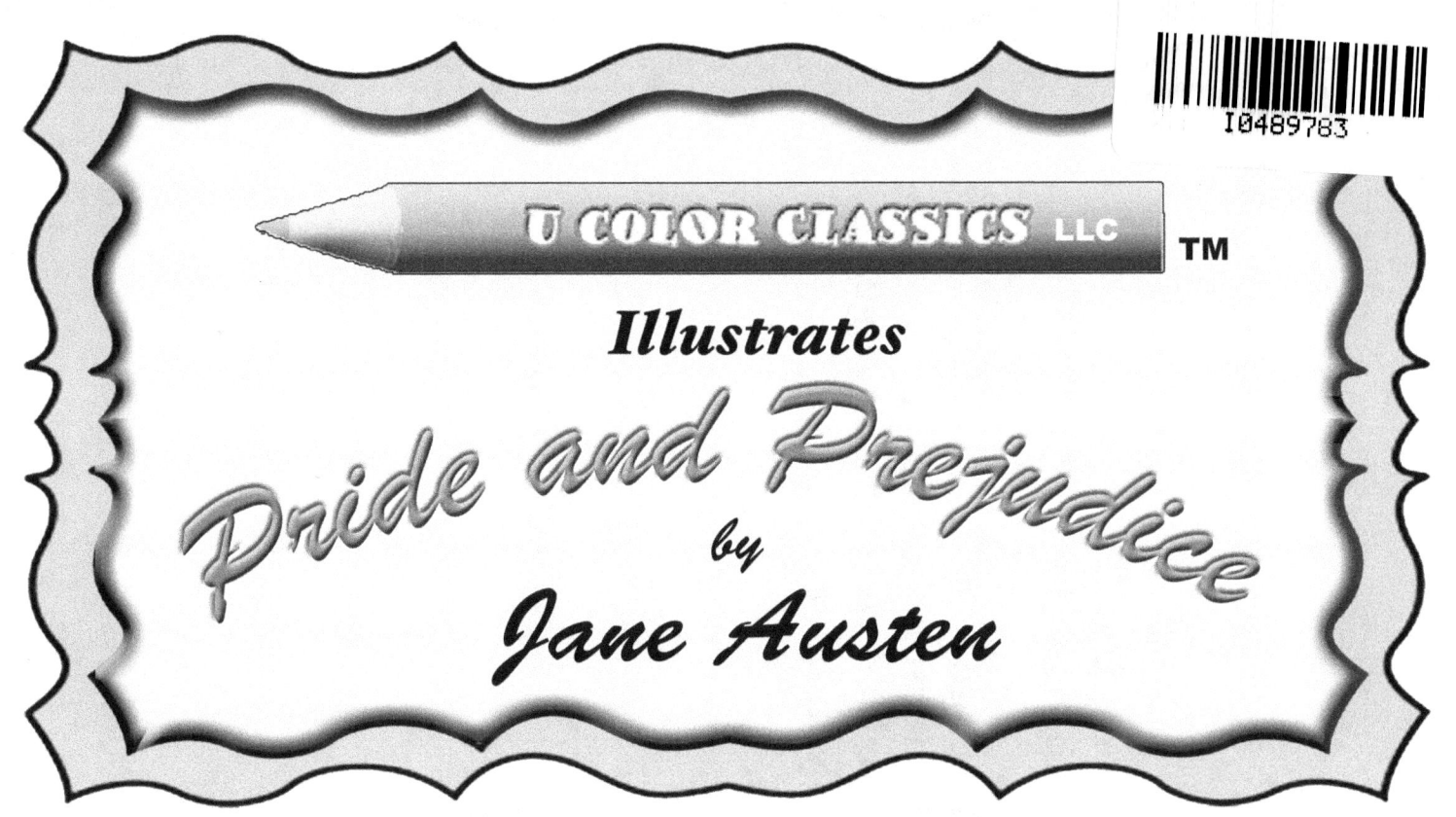

U COLOR CLASSICS LLC ™

Illustrates

Pride and Prejudice

by

Jane Austen

In this book we continue our practice of combining black and white photographic backgrounds with hand drawn characters and animals. The amount of detail makes our books complex but each page is test colored by a 70 year old piano teacher with no previous artistic experience. The end will justify the extra effort. When finished you will have a book of realistic paintings that you will be proud to sign. If you have trouble with any page, please visit our website at *ucolorclassics.com* and look up that page on the **Pride and Prejudice** page. Click on the page you need help with and another page will appear. On it will be an enlarged version of the page you need help with, colorized. It should answer any questions you might have. We hope you get as much satisfaction from colorizing this book as we got from creating it!

Mrs. Bennet tells her daughters the exciting news.
A wealthy young bachelor has just moved into a nearby estate.

Cover

Some of these pages are very complex.
If you need help just go to
ucolorclassics.com.
On the Pride and Prejudice page
look up the page you have questions about and click on it.
The next page you see will be an enlarged, colorized view of that page.
It should answer any questions you have.

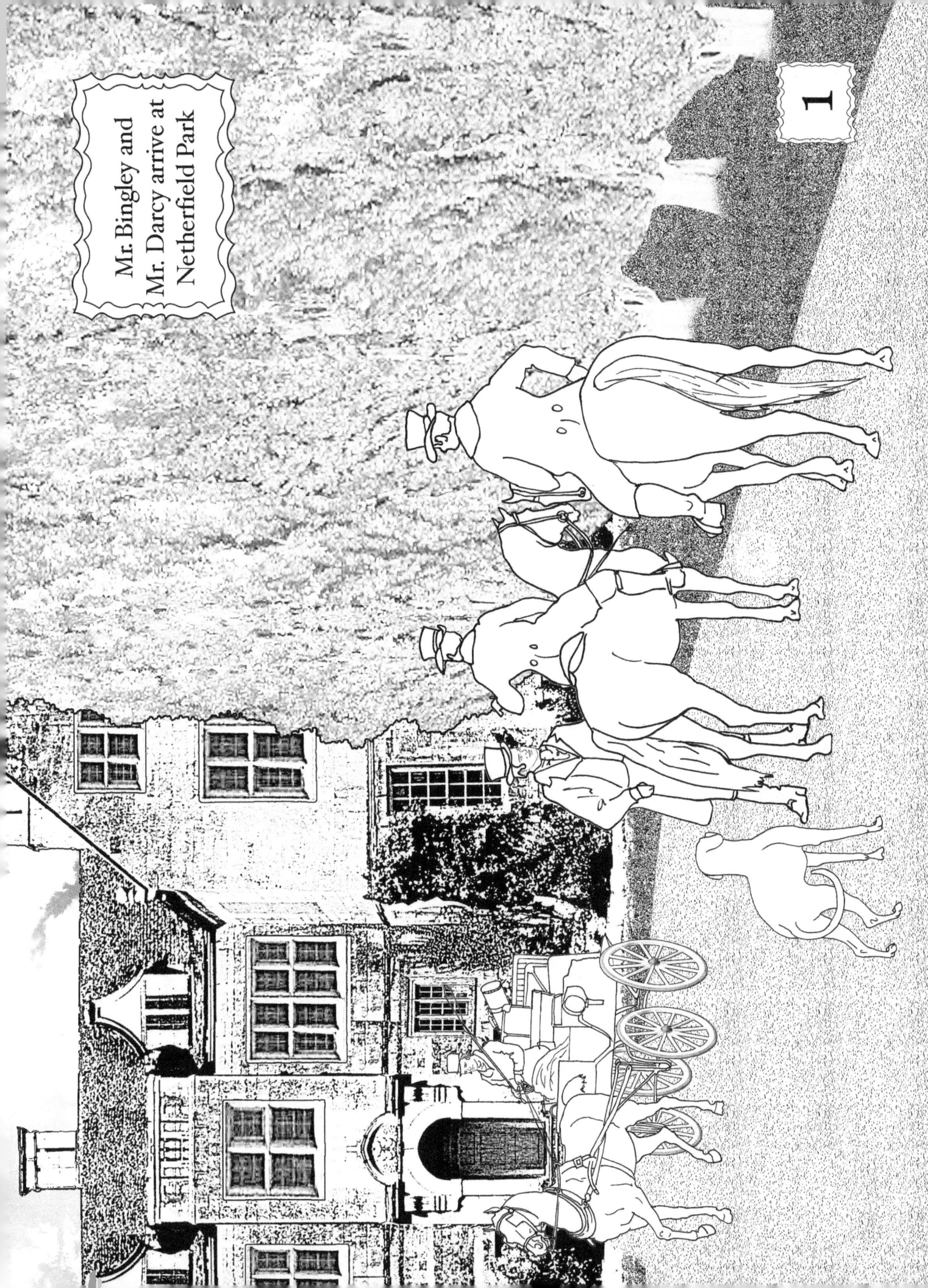

Mr. Bingley and
Mr. Darcy arrive at
Netherfield Park

1

The stone wall is made up of lots of subtly different colored stones decorated with a rose garland. There should be a yellow glow around the candles.

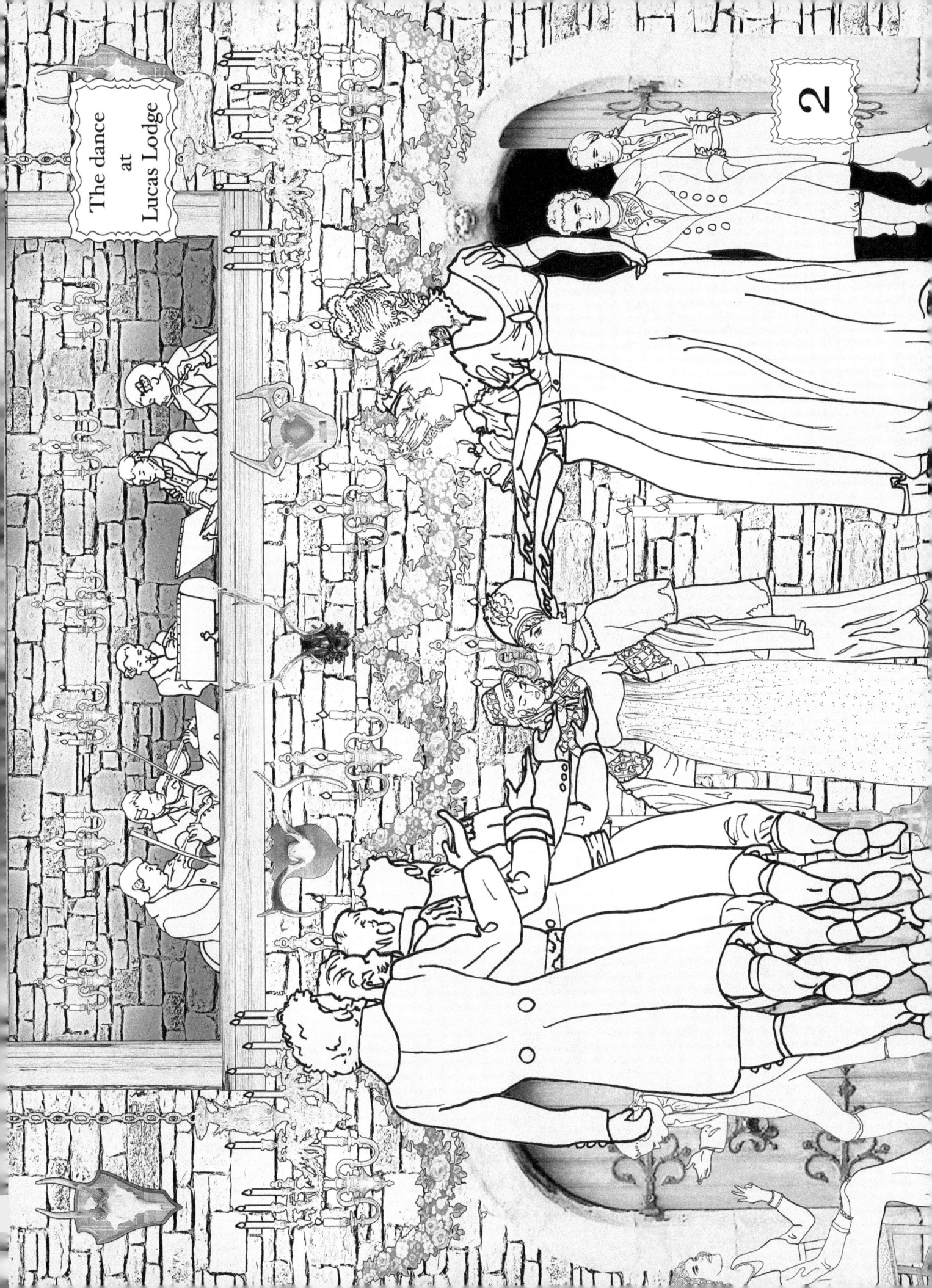

The dance
at
Lucas Lodge

2

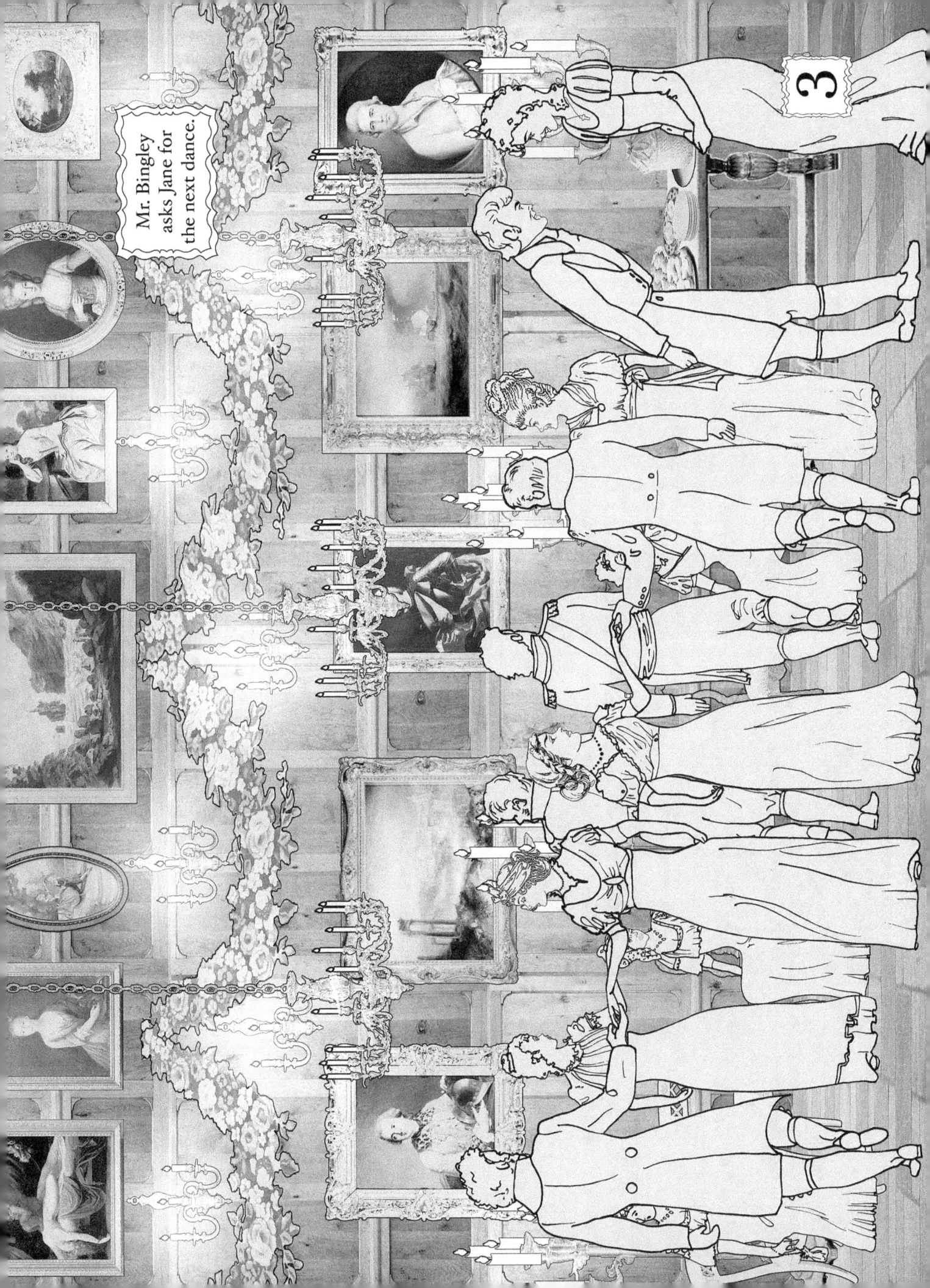

Mr. Bingley asks Jane for the next dance.

3

You've got this one.

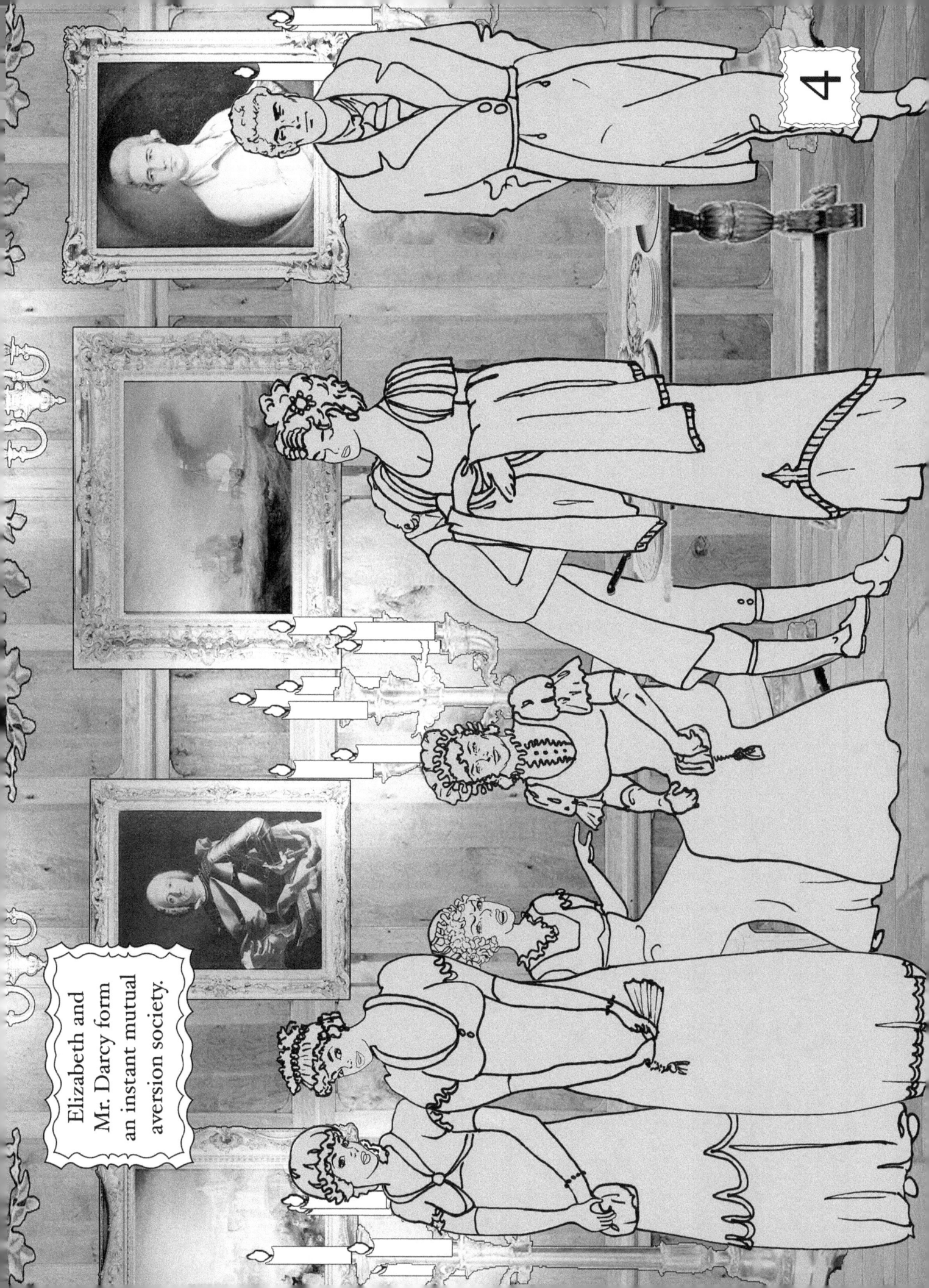

Elizabeth and Mr. Darcy form an instant mutual aversion society.

4

You've got this one too.

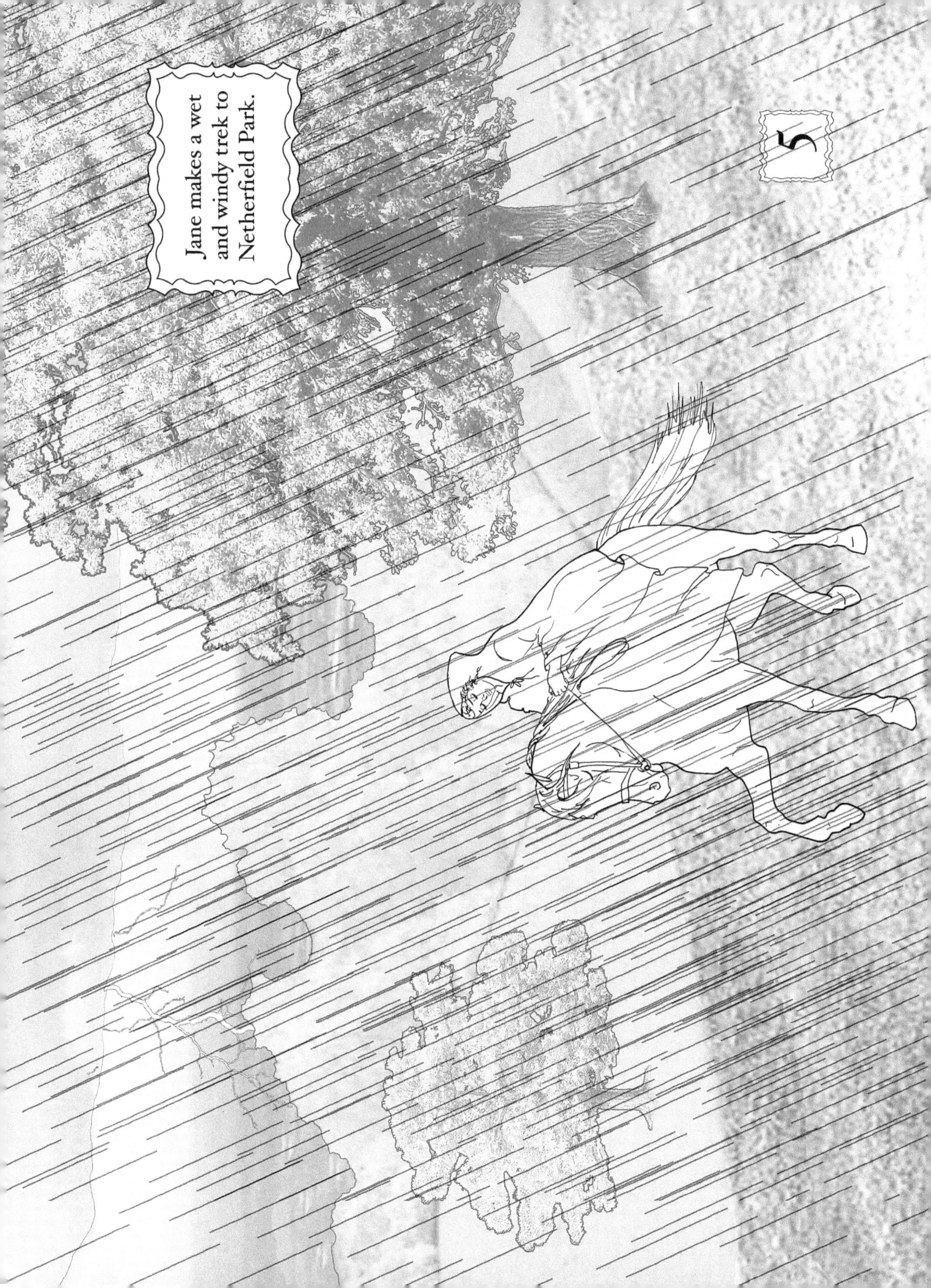

Jane makes a wet and windy trek to Netherfield Park.

5

There is one thing to watch for on this one. In the center there is a distant view of the top of Netherfield Park. Check page one to see the colors you used. There is also a patch of sky above the roof and below the foliage.

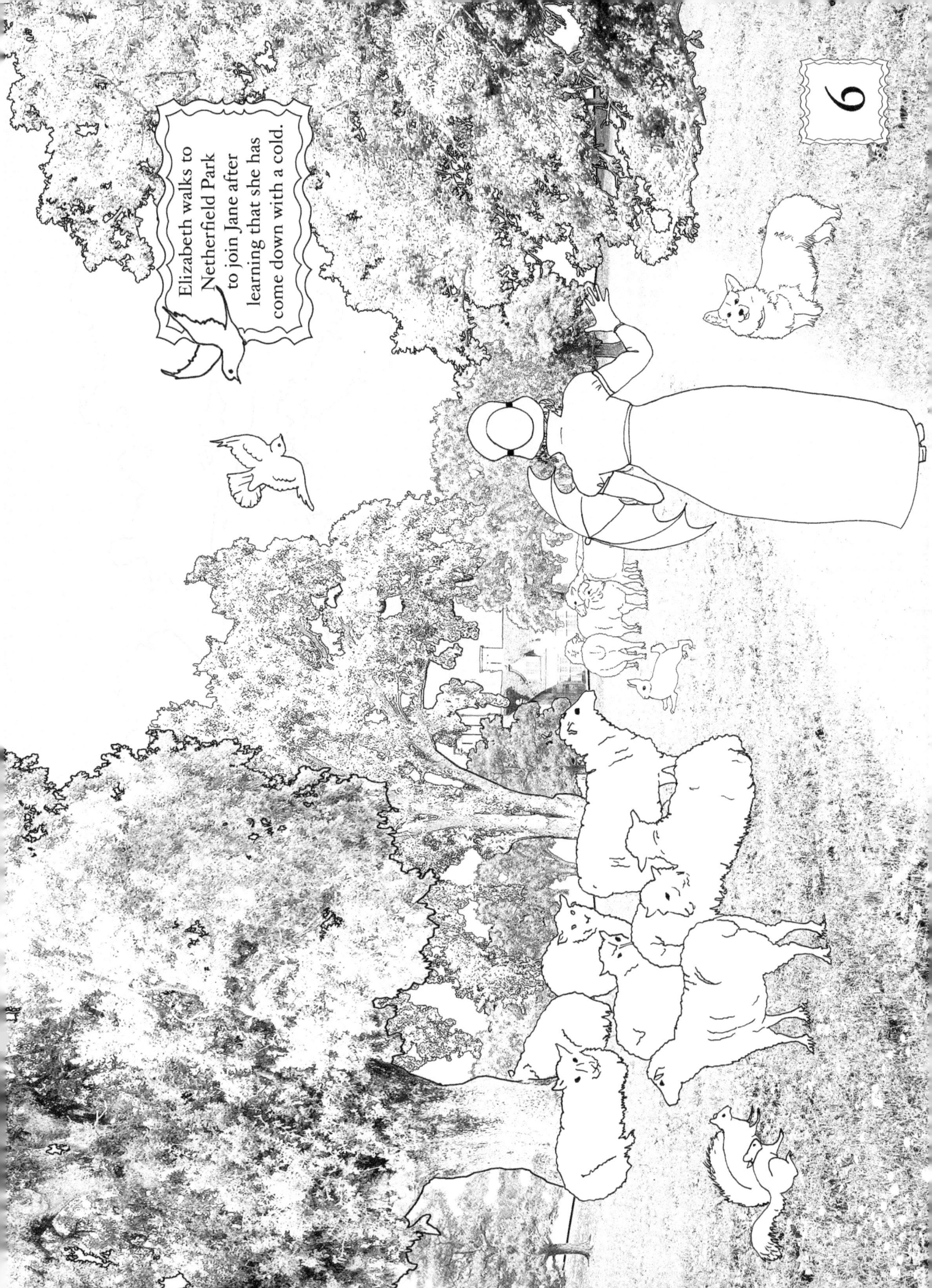

Elizabeth walks to Netherfield Park to join Jane after learning that she has come down with a cold.

6

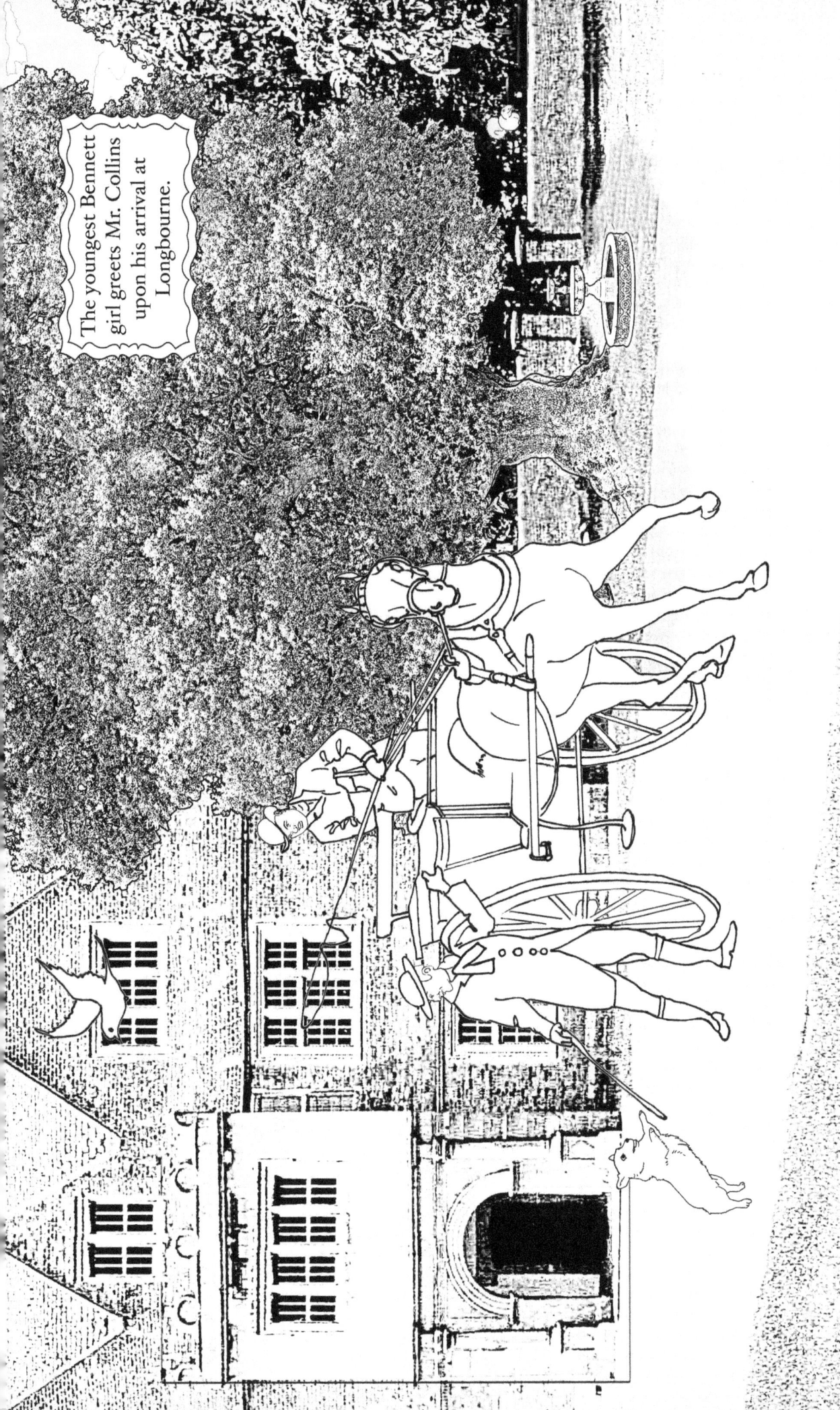

The youngest Bennett girl greets Mr. Collins upon his arrival at Longbourne.

7

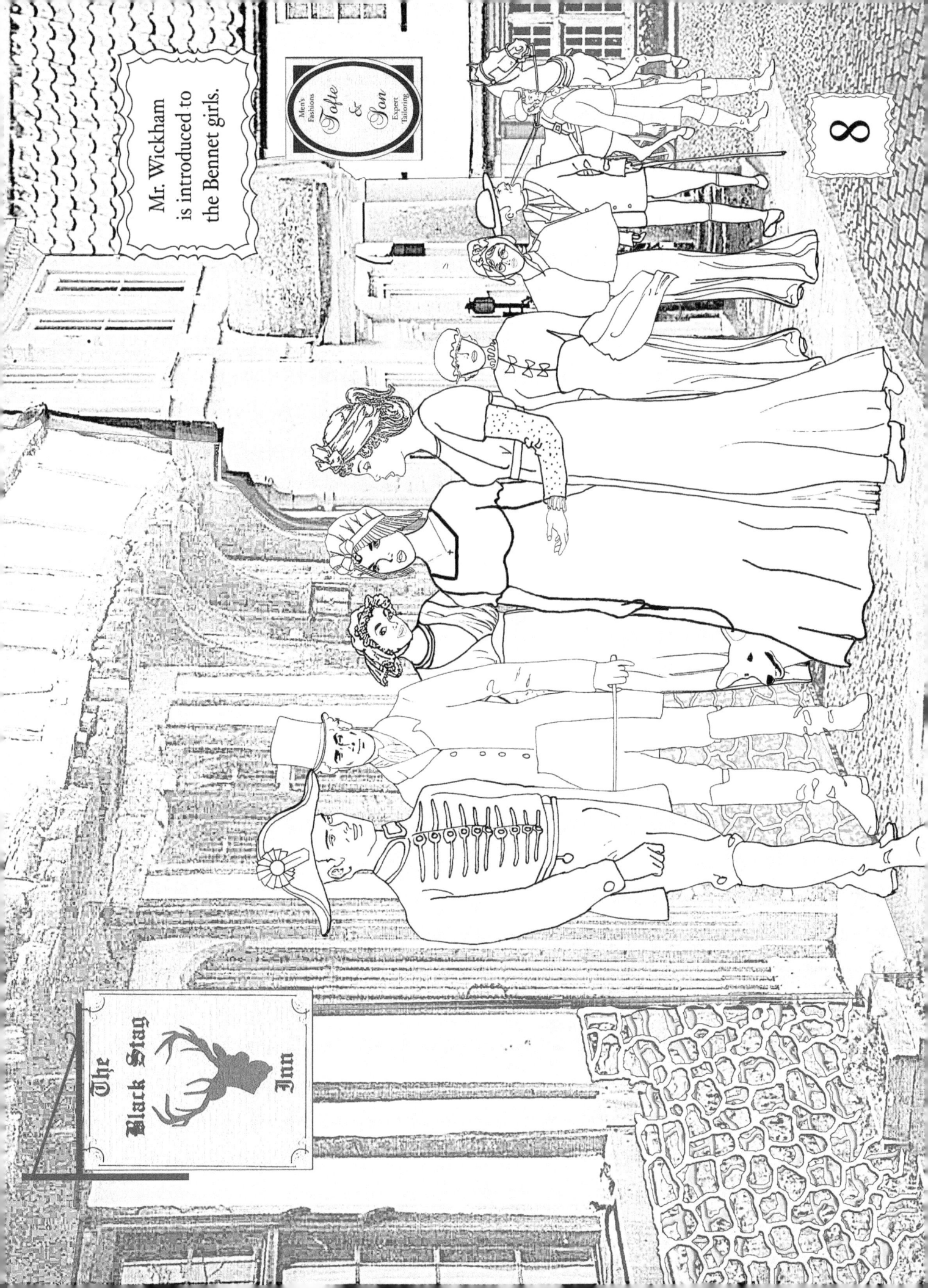

Mr. Wickham is introduced to the Bennet girls.

Men's Fashions
Tofte & Son
Expert Tailoring

The Black Stag Inn

8

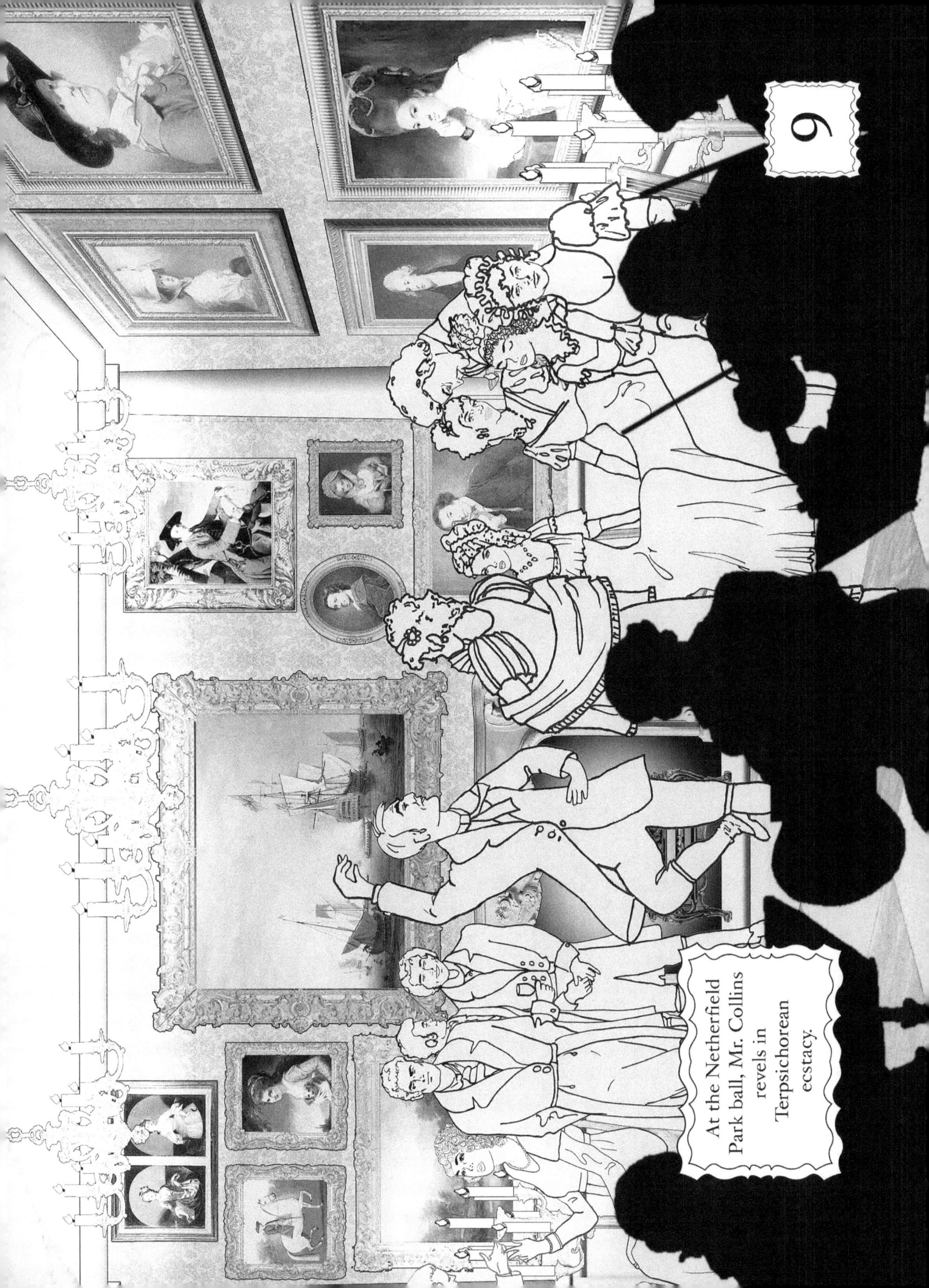

9

At the Netherfield Park ball, Mr. Collins revels in Terpsichorean ecstacy.

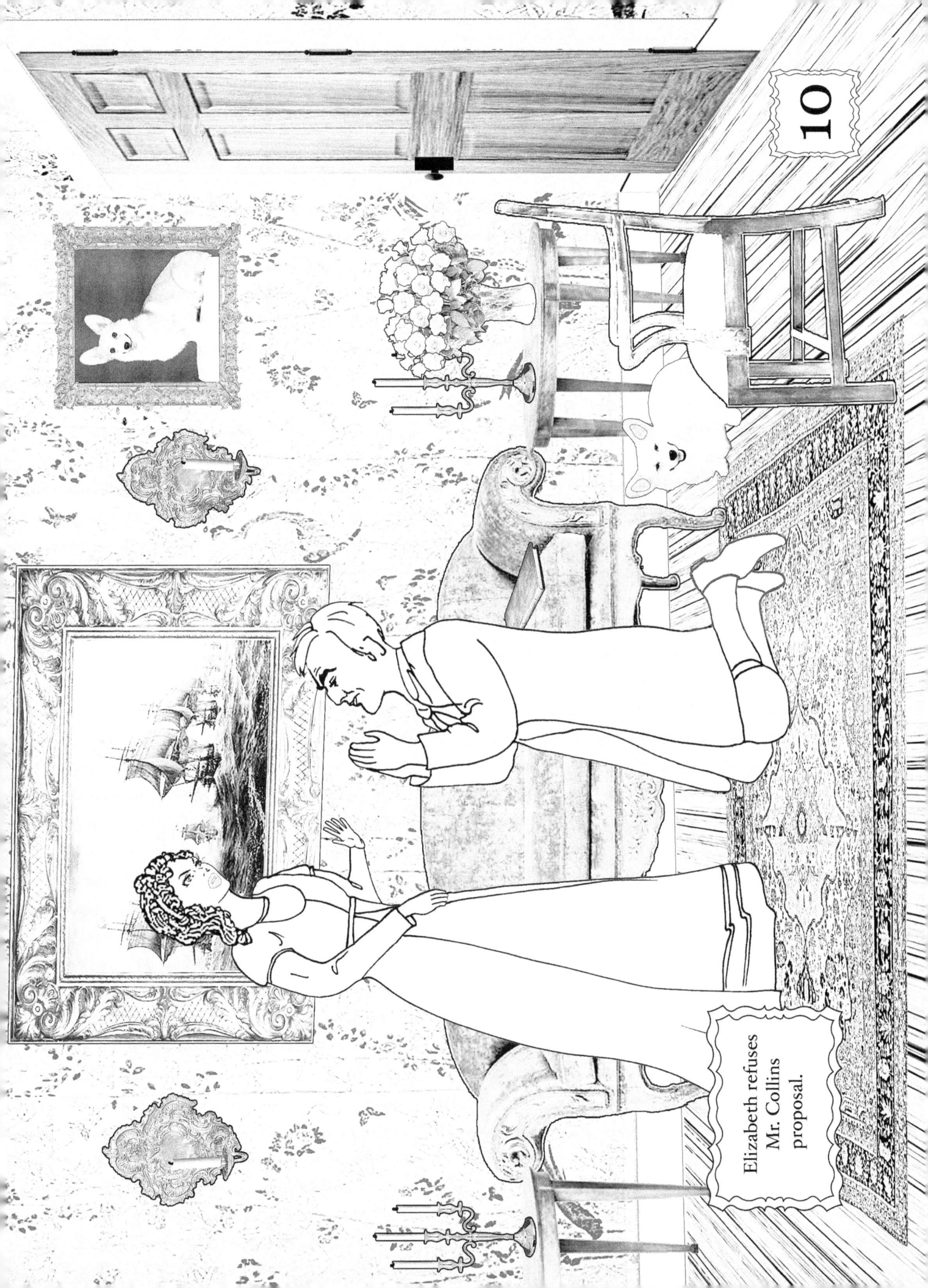

Elizabeth refuses Mr. Collins proposal.

10

Imagine the fragrance!

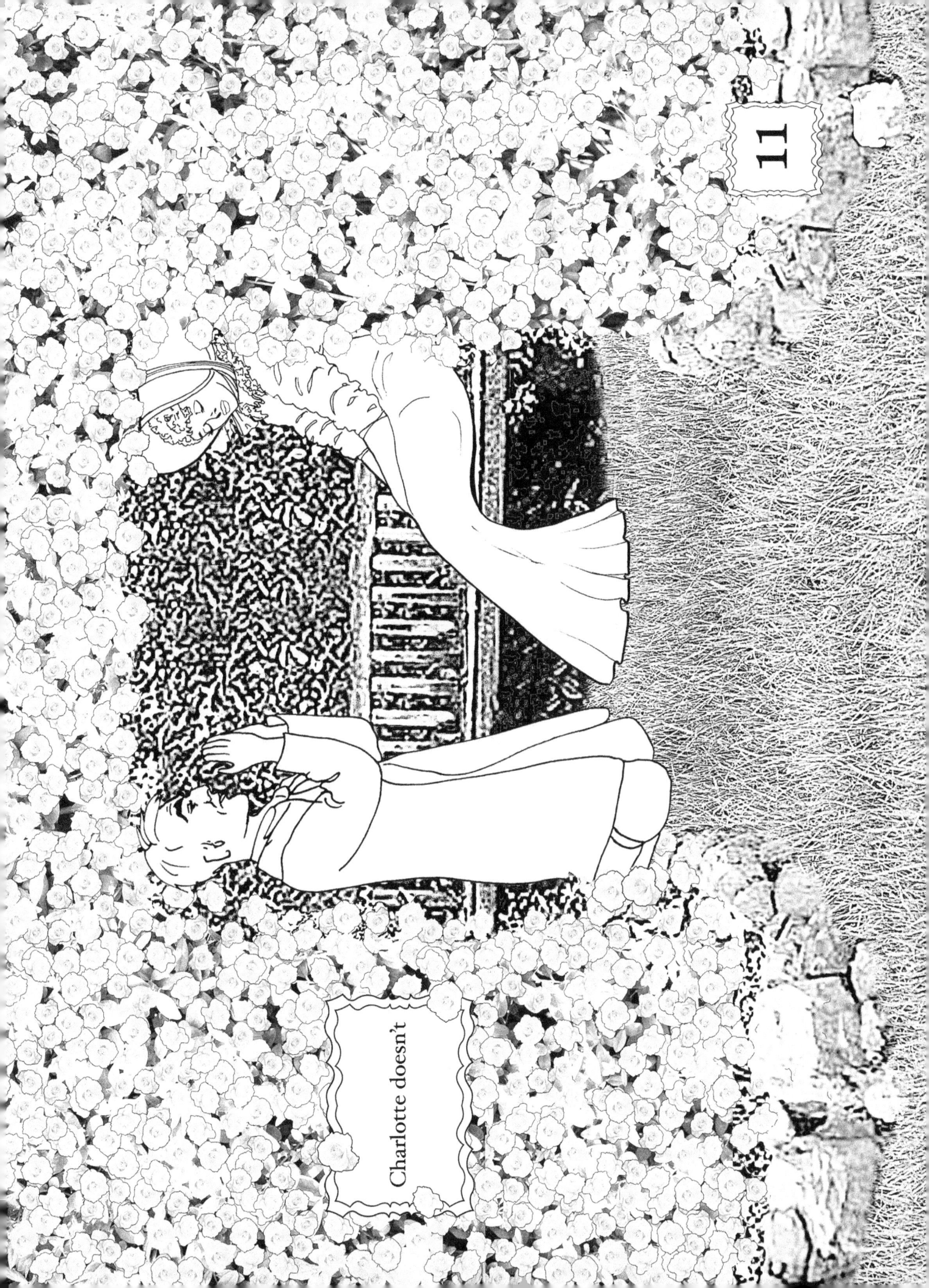

Slightly different perspective than page one.

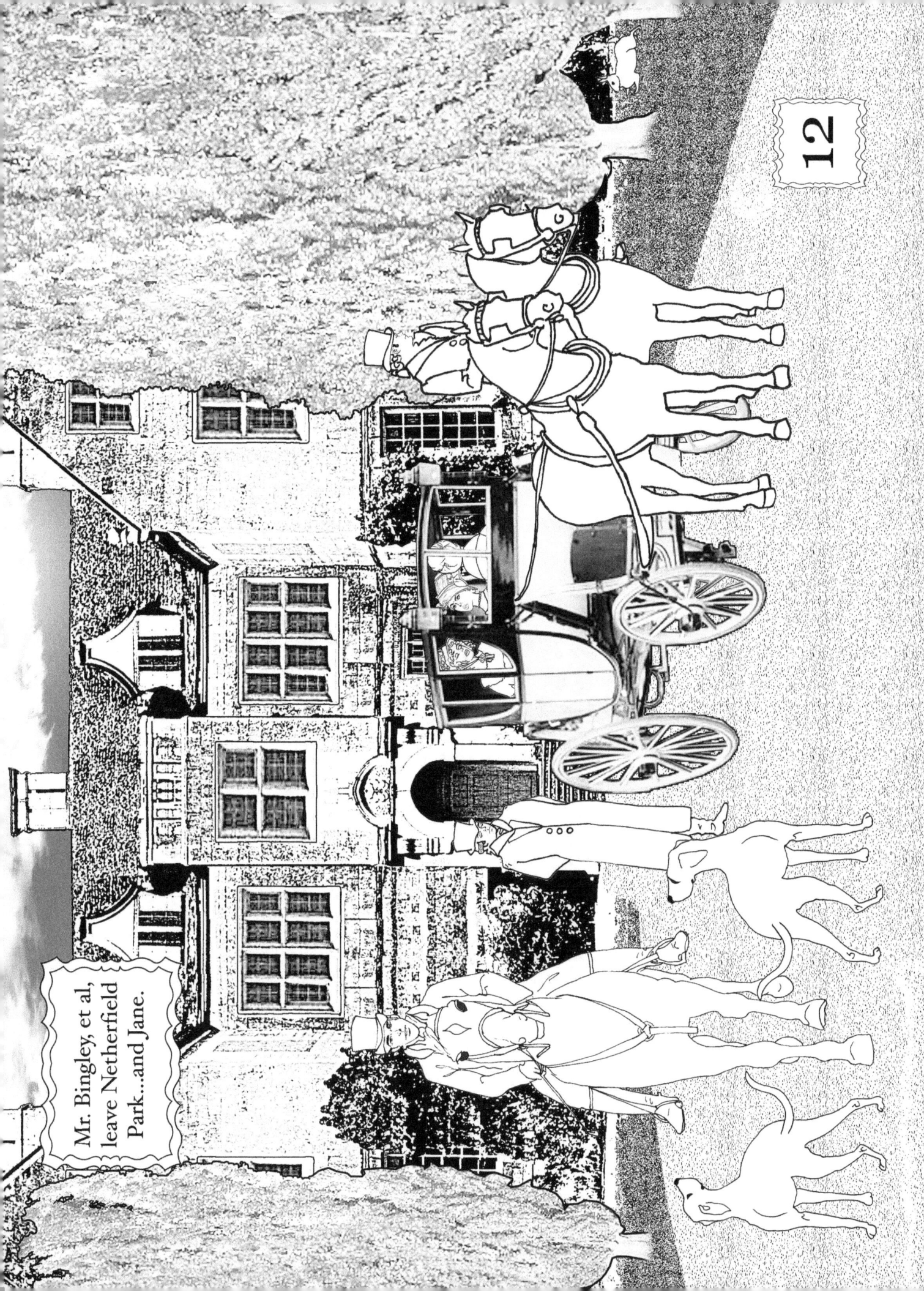

Mr. Bingley, et al, leave Netherfield Park...and Jane.

12

Use a variety of different shades of the same color for the bricks.

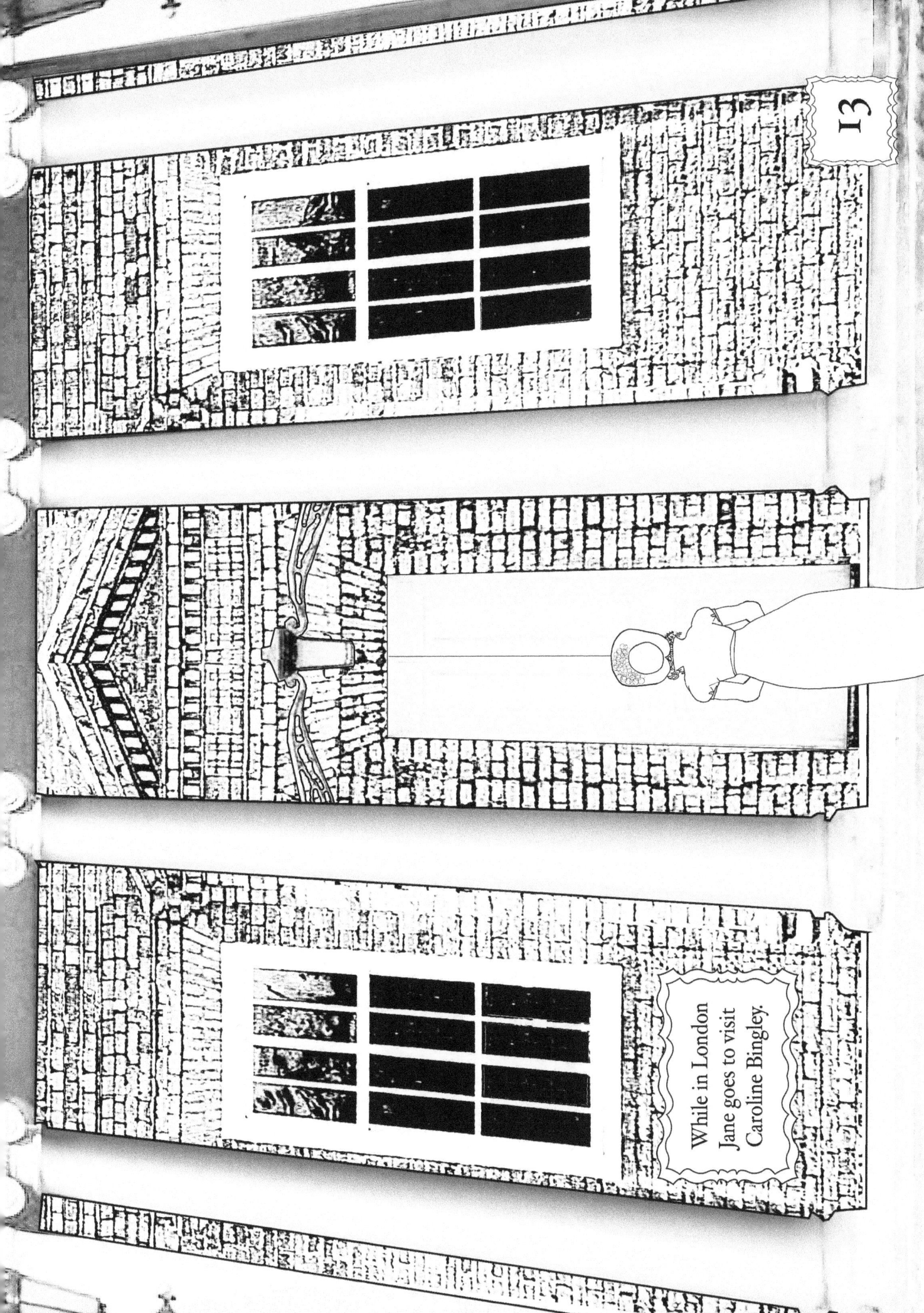

While in London
Jane goes to visit
Caroline Bingley.

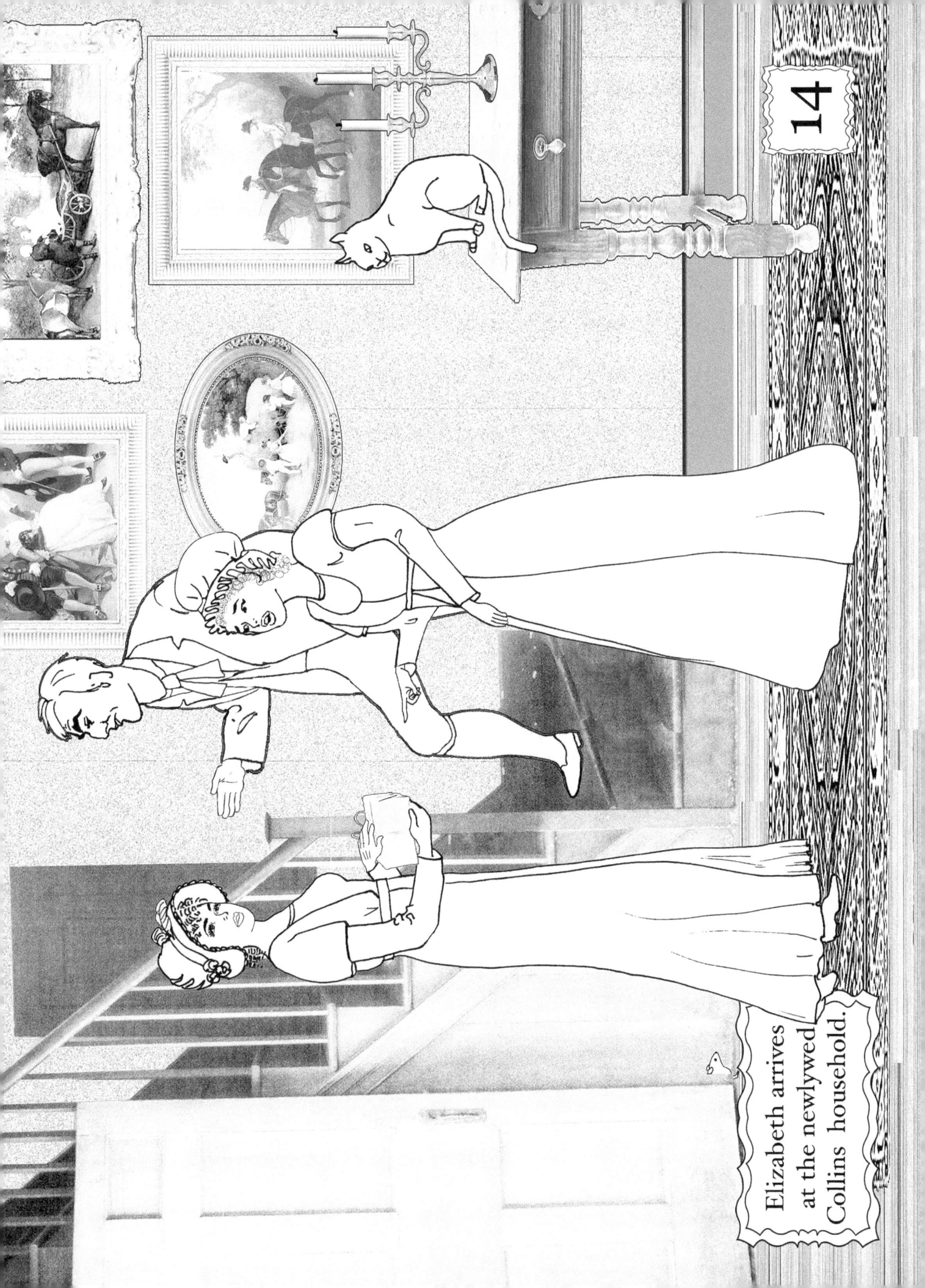

Elizabeth arrives at the newlywed Collins household.

14

Have fun!

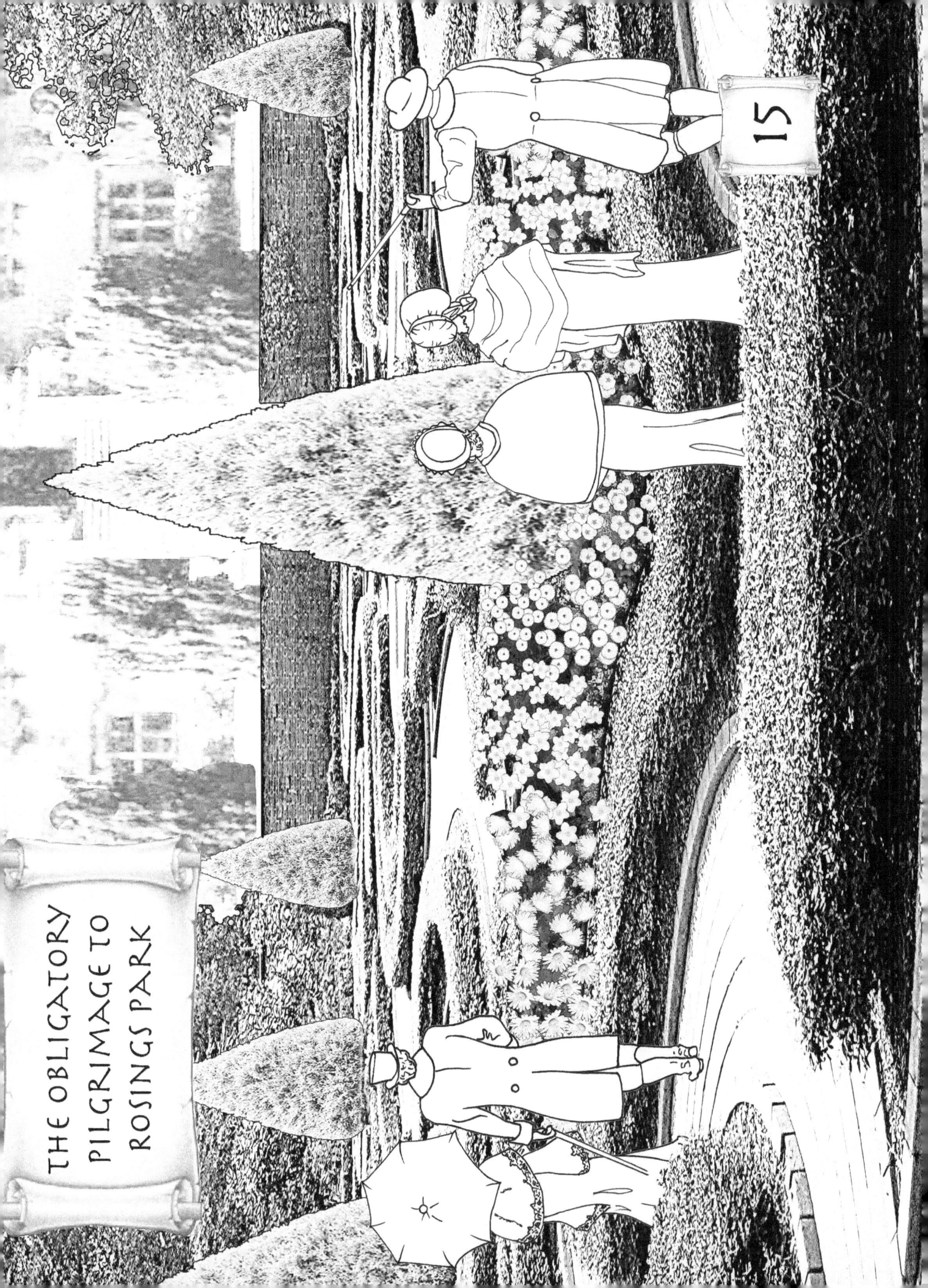

THE OBLIGATORY PILGRIMAGE TO ROSINGS PARK

15

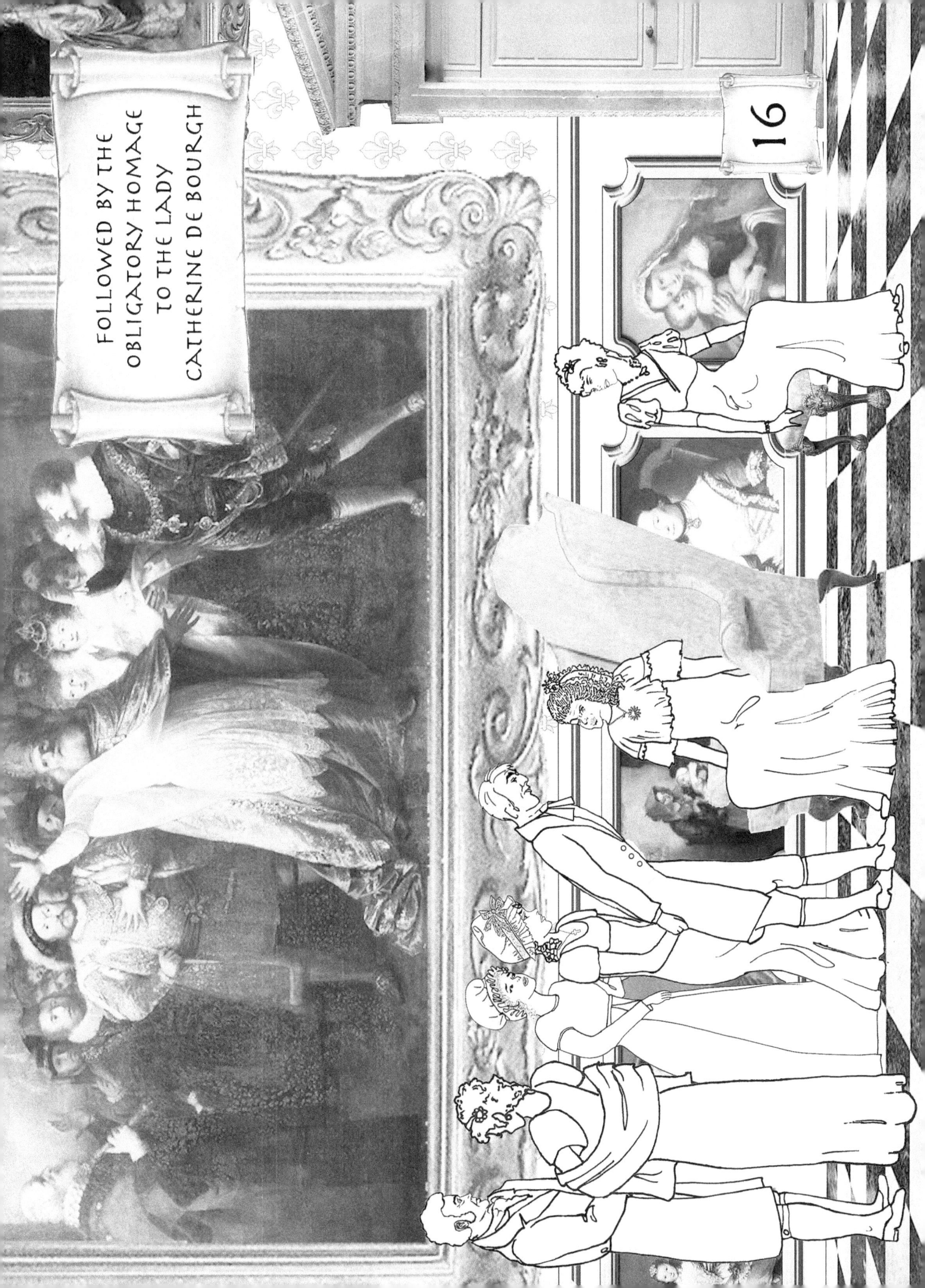

FOLLOWED BY THE
OBLIGATORY HOMAGE
TO THE LADY
CATHERINE DE BOURGH

16

The scene outside looks distorted because it's cheap glass. Those are water stains near the window frames. The Collins house needs work.

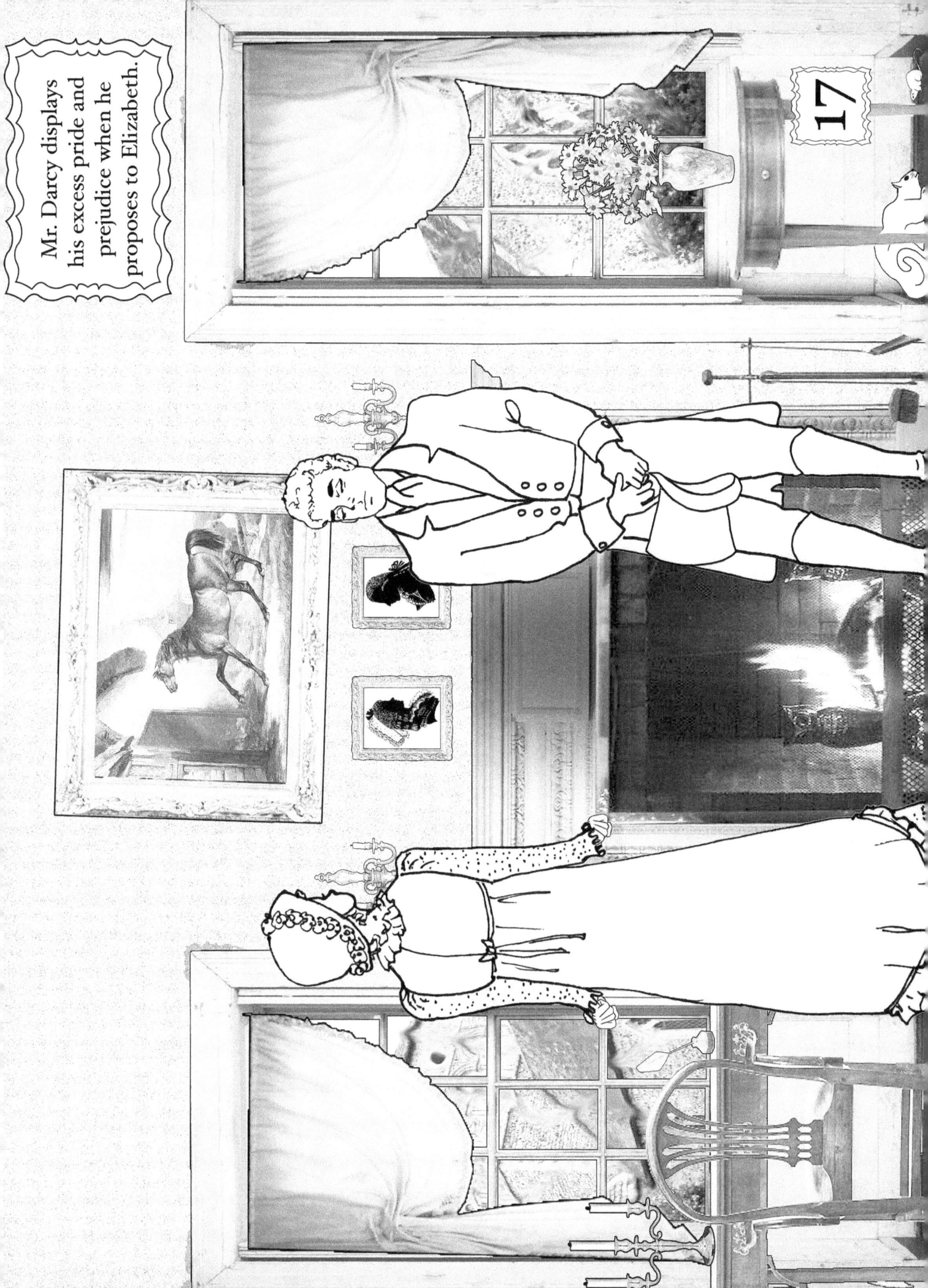

Mr. Darcy displays his excess pride and prejudice when he proposes to Elizabeth.

17

Broad strokes + busy work = beautiful landscape.

18

Elizabeth reads Darcy's letter and learns of Wickham's deceitful nature.

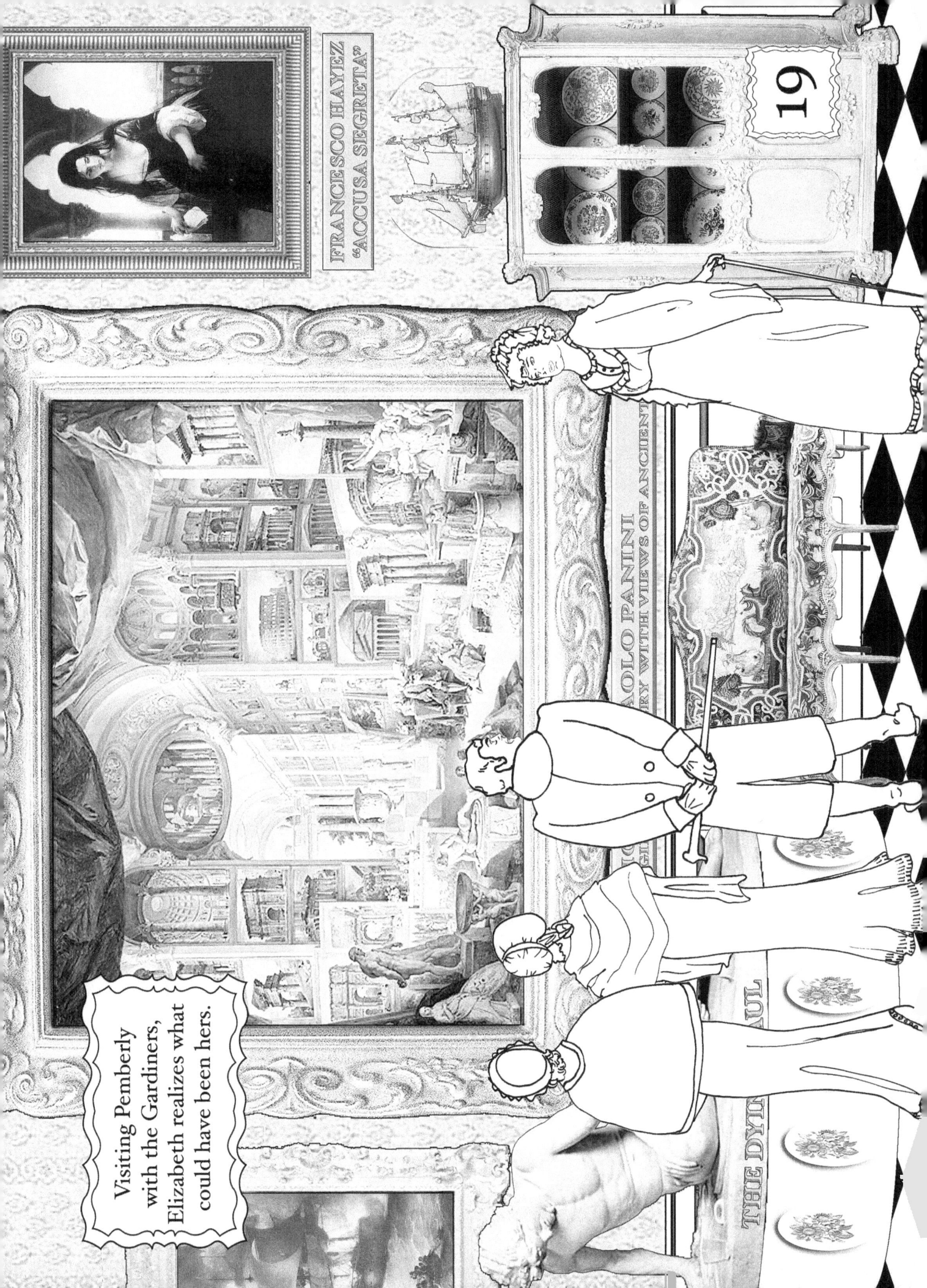

FRANCESCO HAYEZ
"ACCUSA SEGRETA"

19

PAOLO PANINI
...RY WITH VIEWS OF ANCIENT...

THE DYIN...

PAUL

Visiting Pemberly
with the Gardiners,
Elizabeth realizes what
could have been hers.

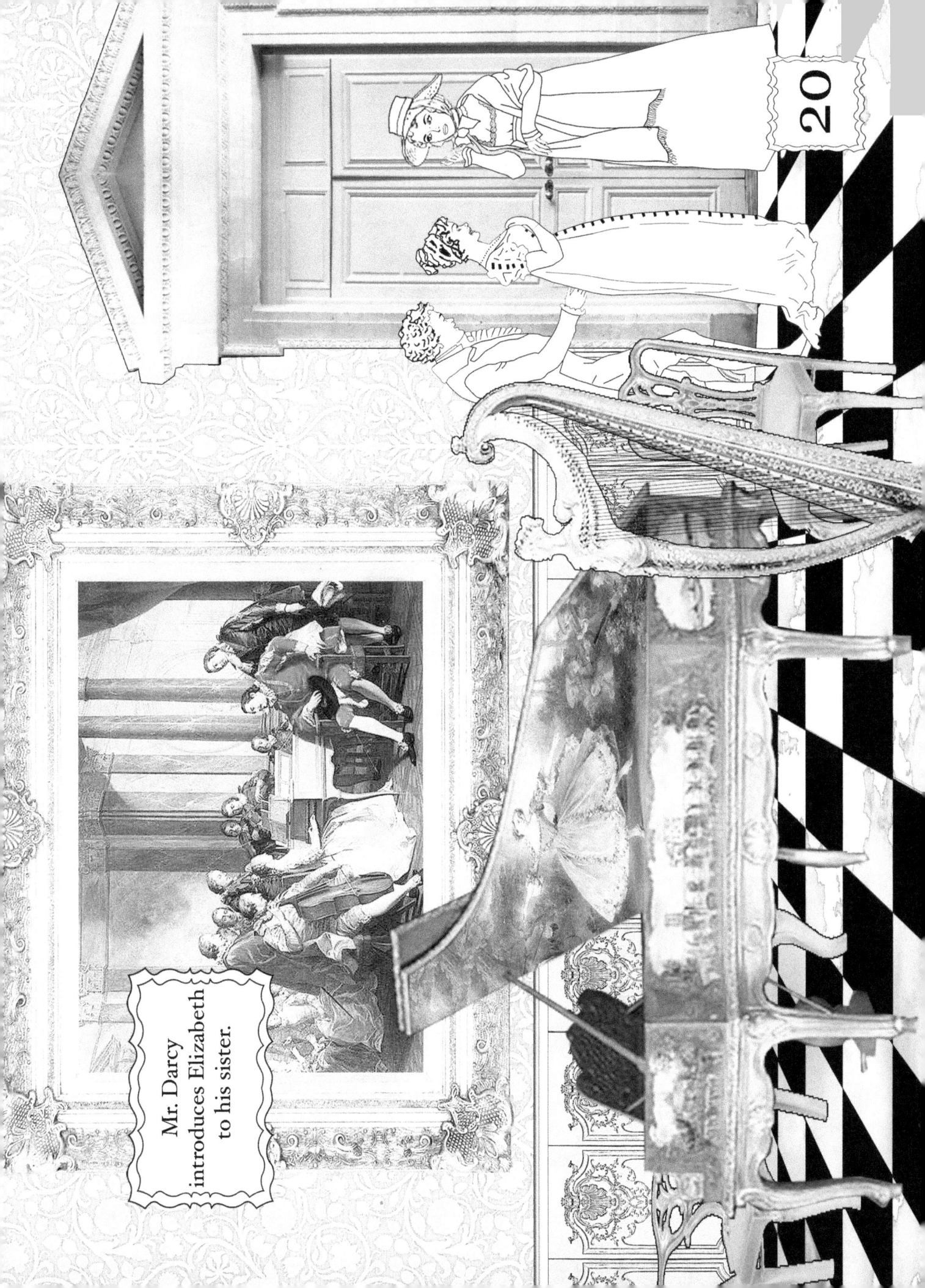

Mr. Darcy
introduces Elizabeth
to his sister.

Lots of little details on this page including five people and one horse out on the street.

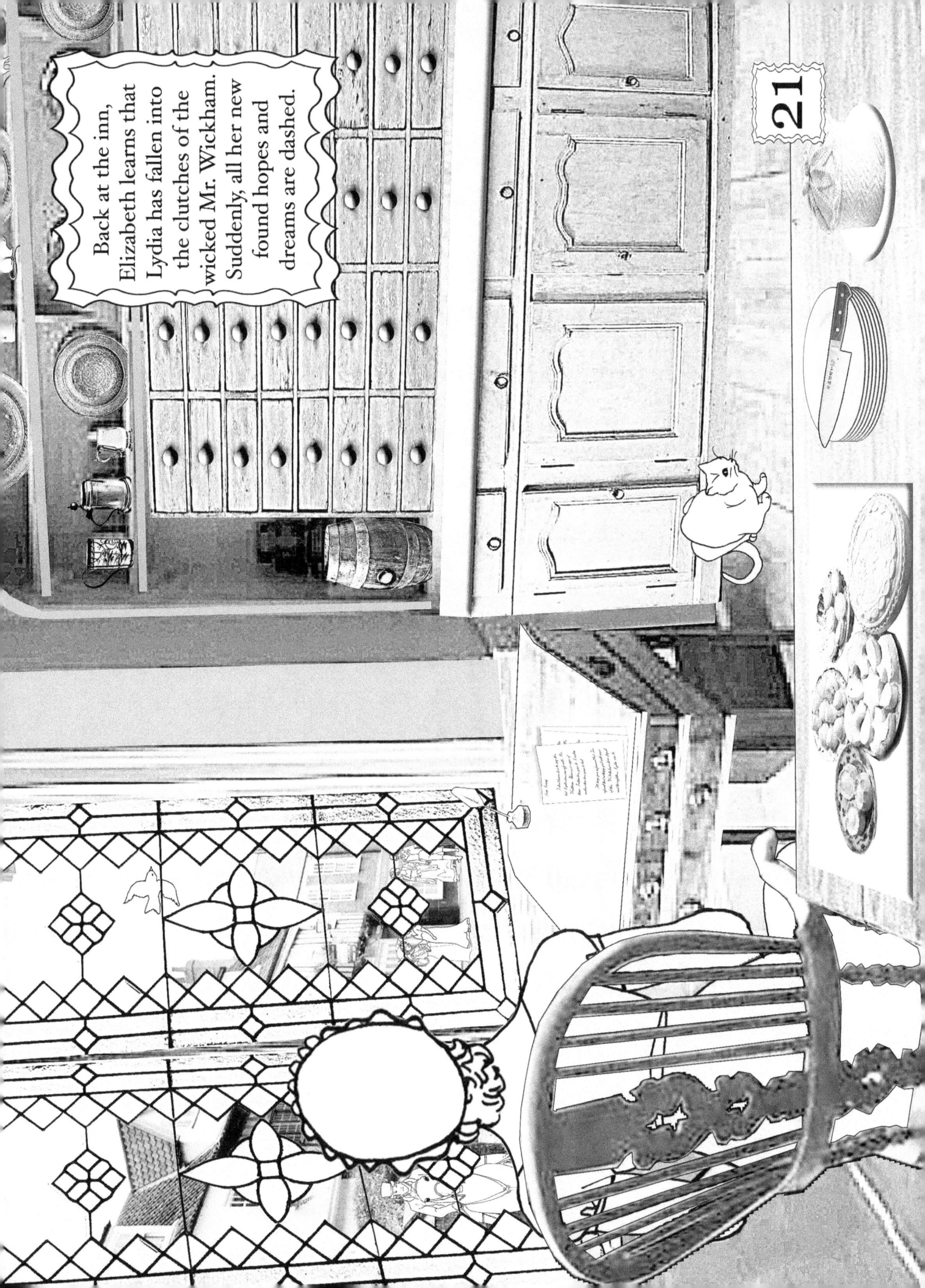

Back at the inn, Elizabeth learns that Lydia has fallen into the clutches of the wicked Mr. Wickham. Suddenly, all her new found hopes and dreams are dashed.

That's an apple orchard on the left side of the house. Do it in green mixed in with various sized clumps of pink. The harvest is on page 28.

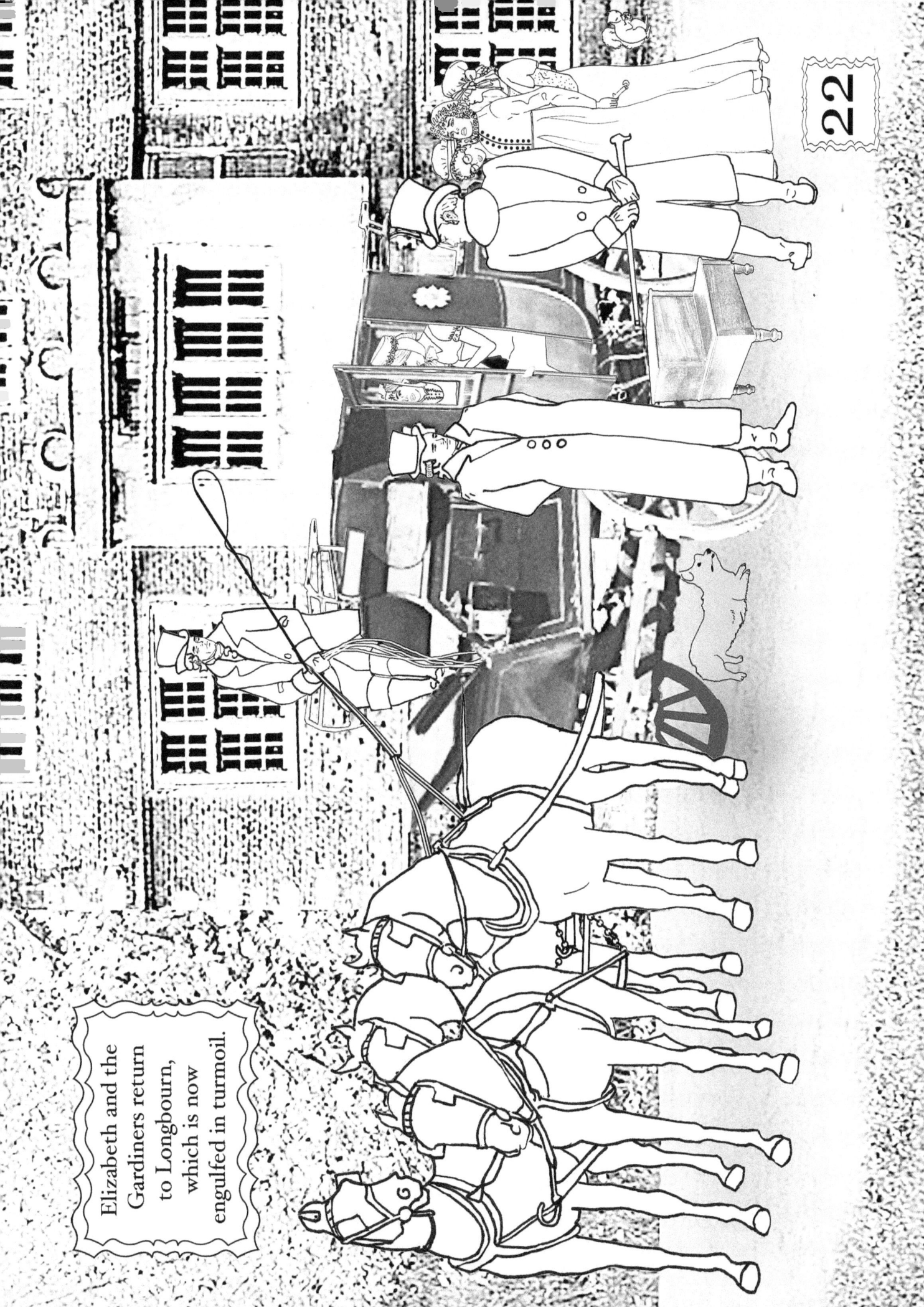

Elizabeth and the Gardiners return to Longbourn, which is now engulfed in turmoil.

22

A pretty little spot.

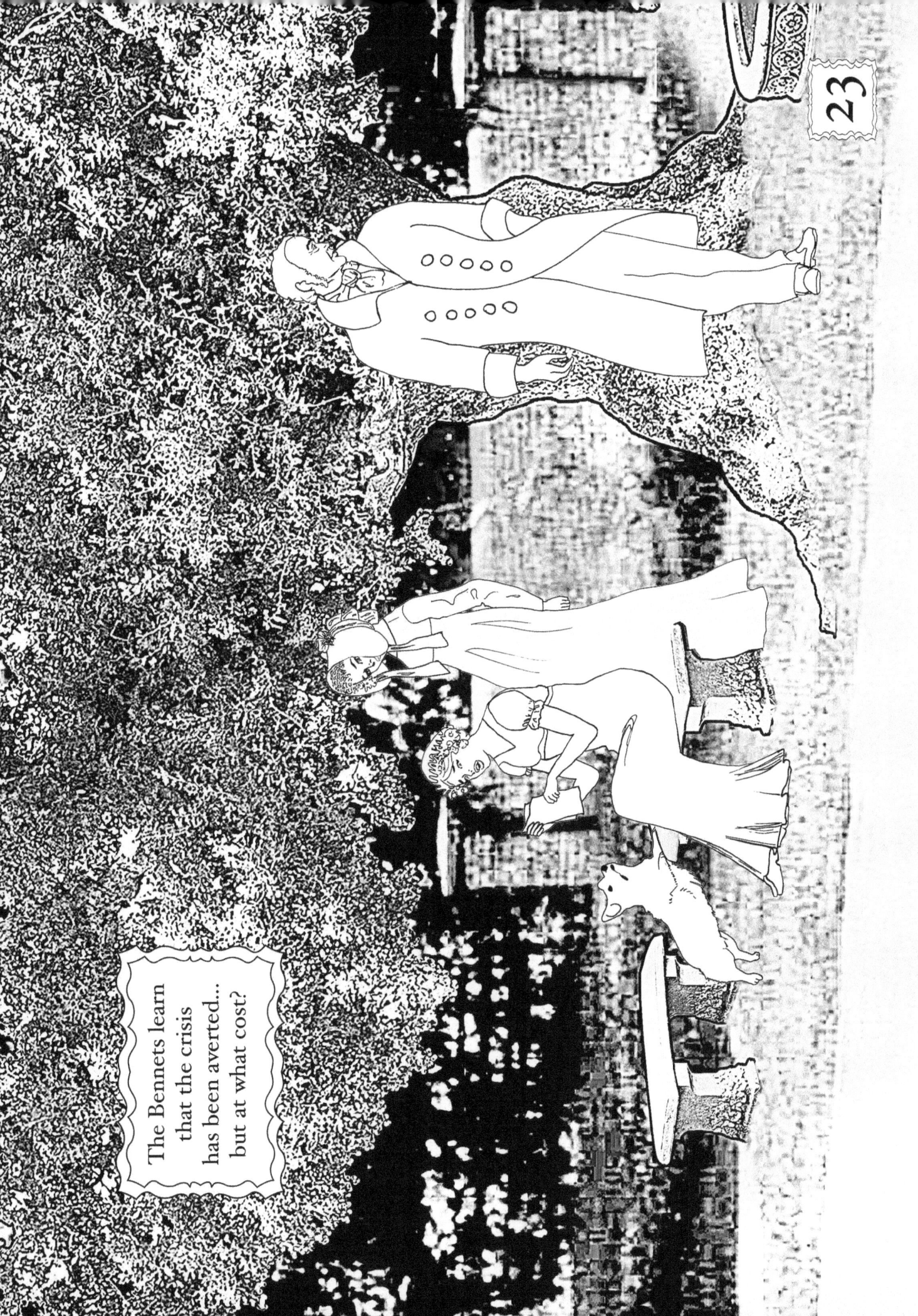

The Bennets learn that the crisis has been averted... but at what cost?

Well, actually, the whole neighborhood is quite nice.

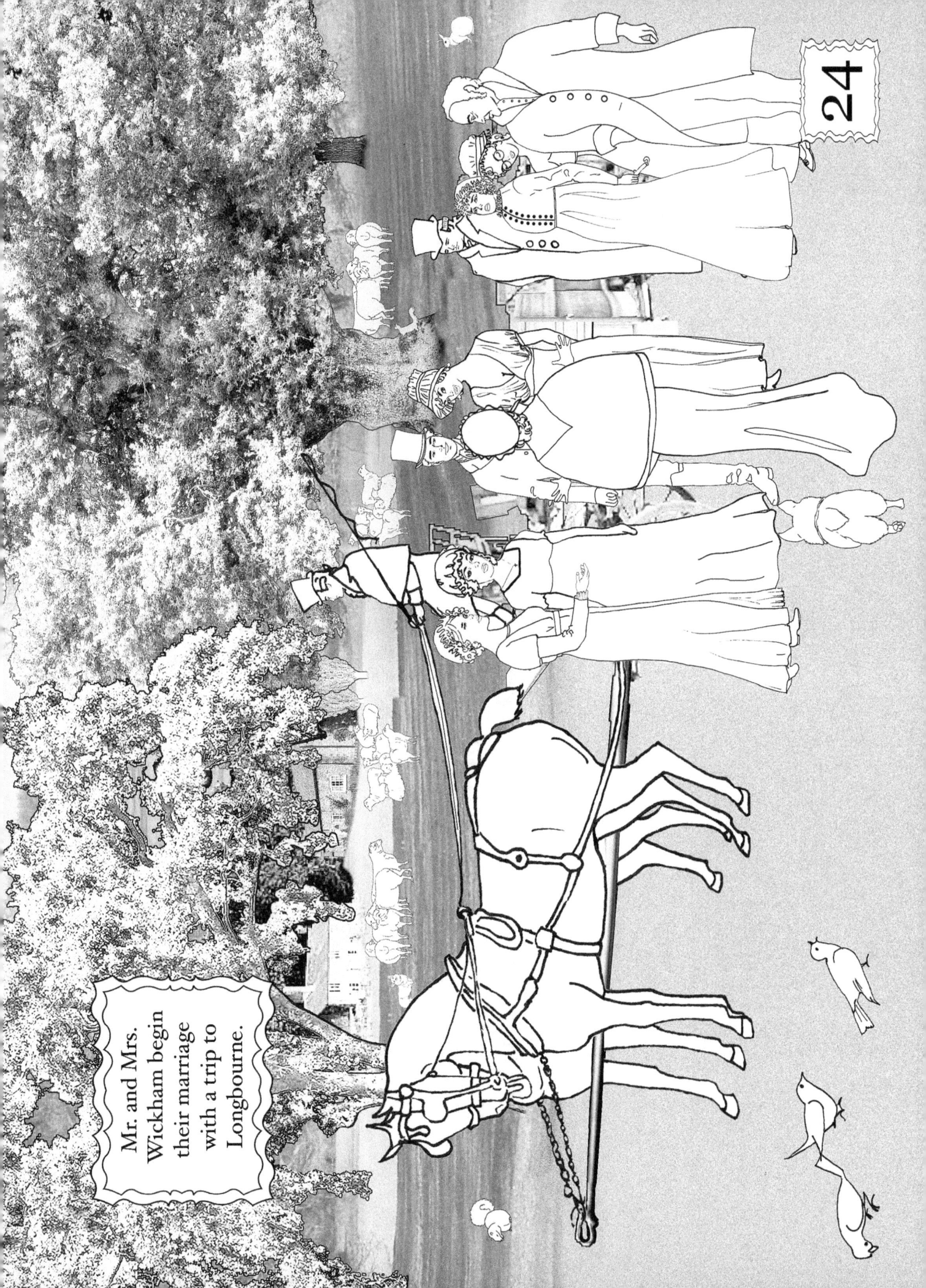

Mr. and Mrs. Wickham begin their marriage with a trip to Longbourne.

24

Longbourne is a family farm. They grow what they eat. That's a garden out back, complete with two bee hives.

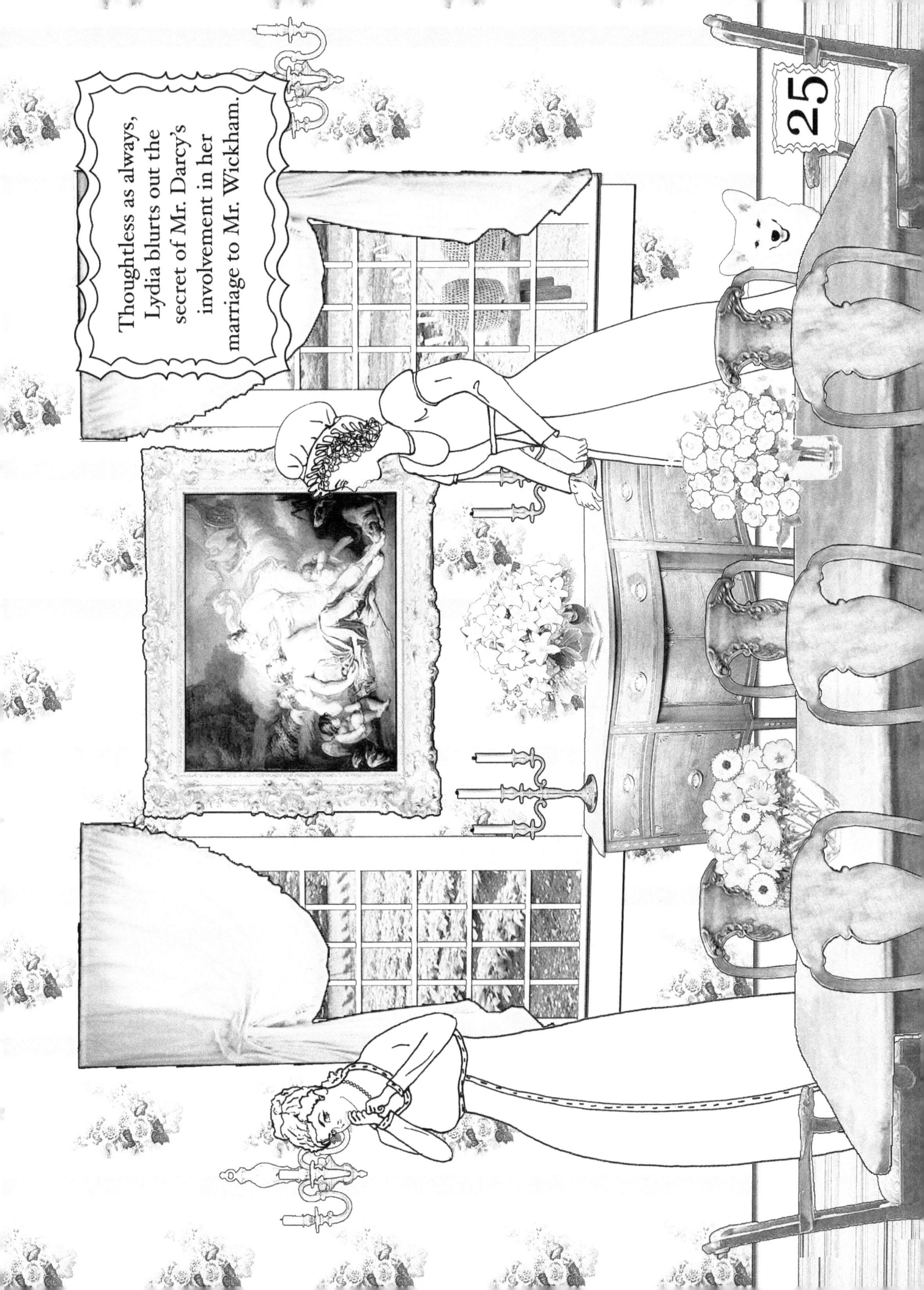

Thoughtless as always, Lydia blurts out the secret of Mr. Darcy's involvement in her marriage to Mr. Wickham.

25

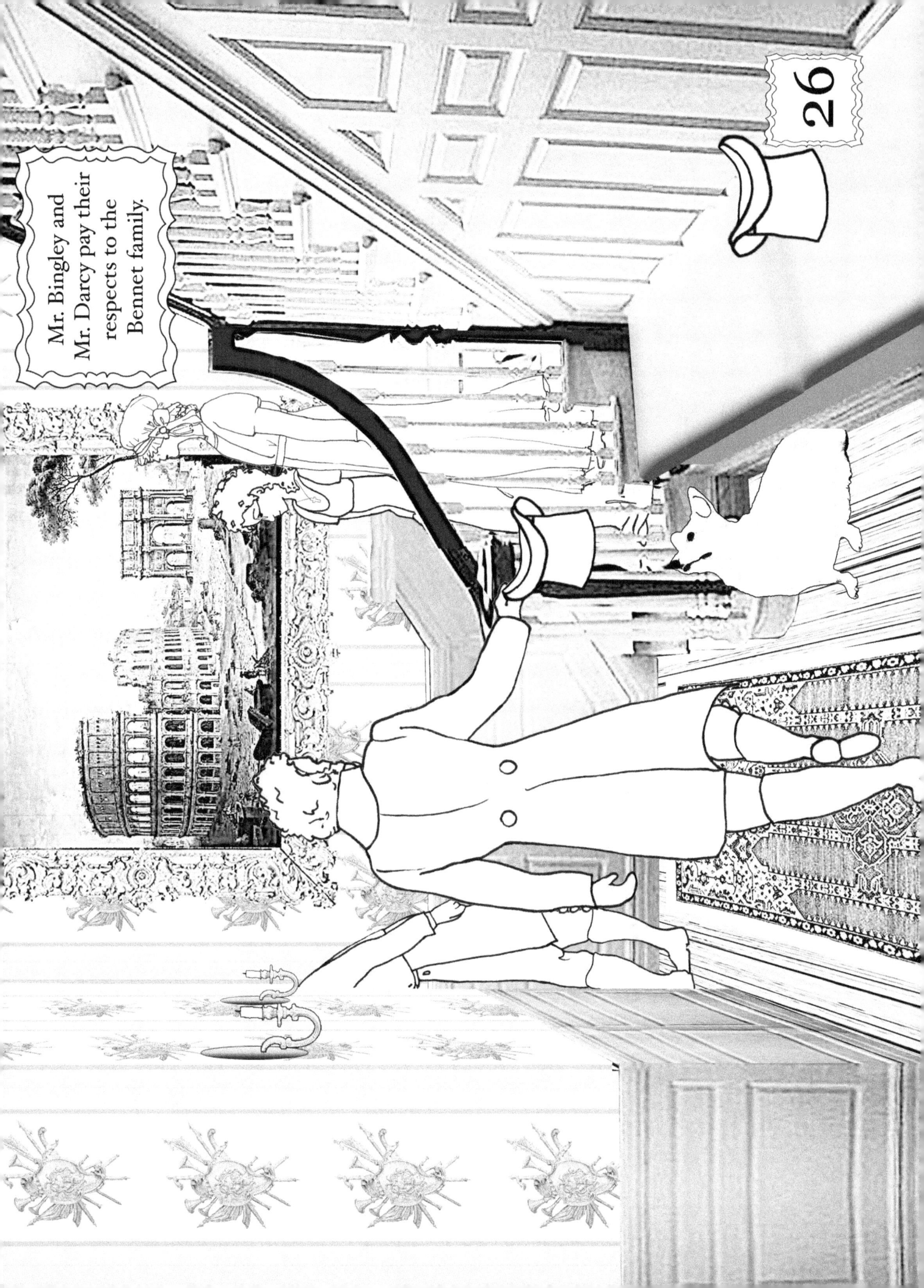

Mr. Bingley and Mr. Darcy pay their respects to the Bennet family.

26

We've seen this room before from a different perspective, both physically and emotionally.

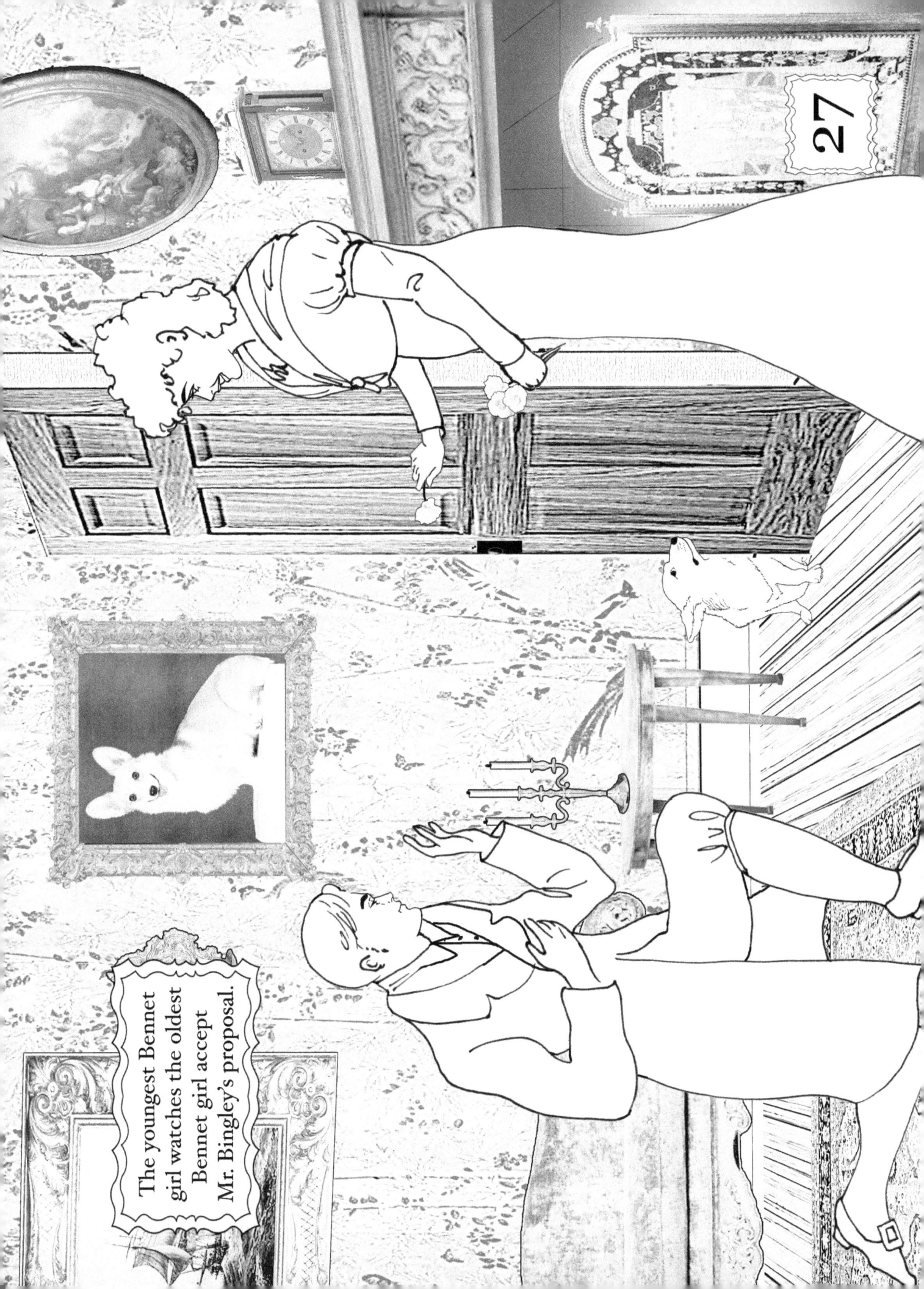

The youngest Bennet girl watches the oldest Bennet girl accept Mr. Bingley's proposal.

Make the apples two tone; red & green.

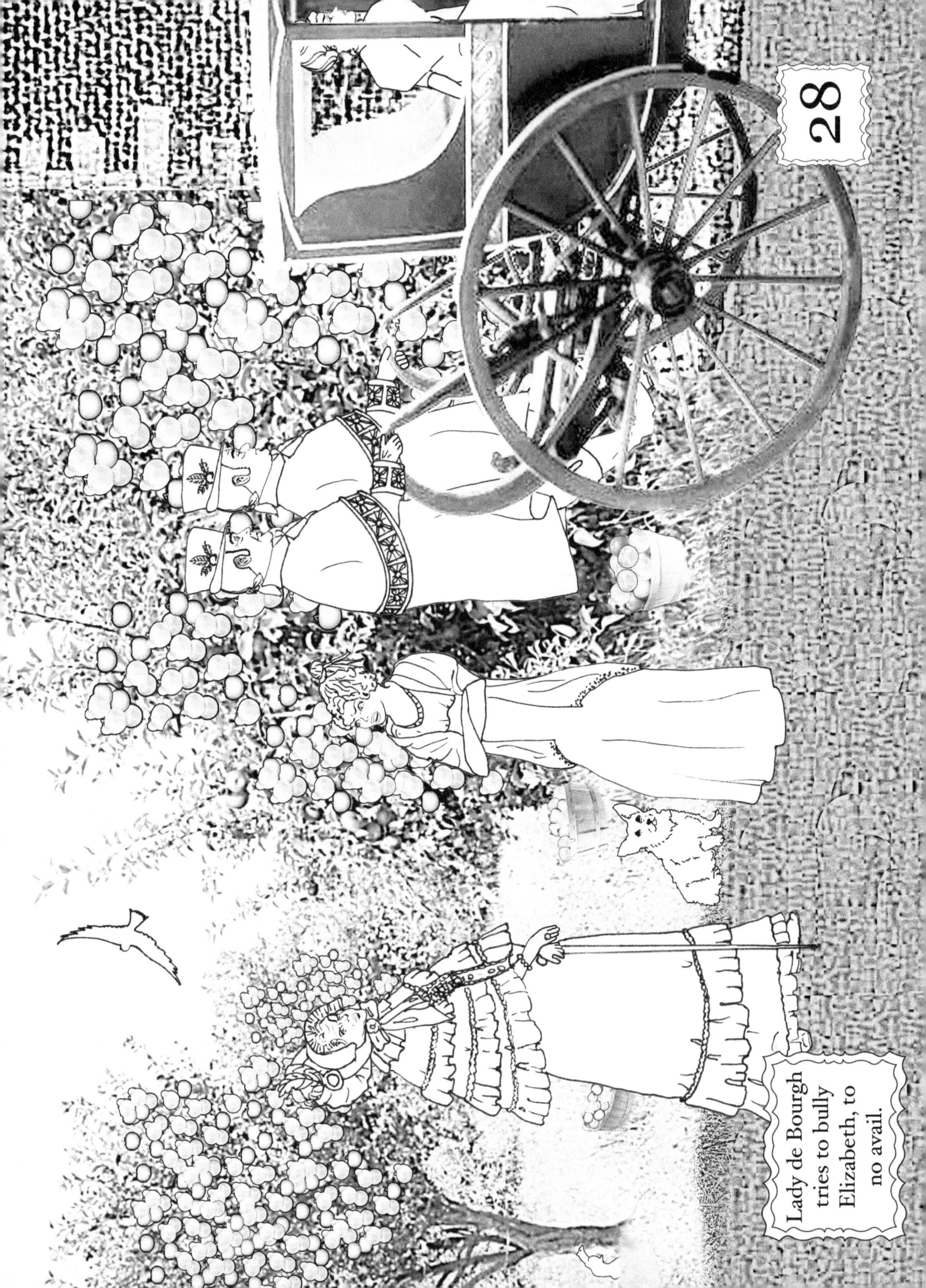

28

Lady de Bourgh tries to bully Elizabeth, to no avail.

There are two birds and a gopher on this page.

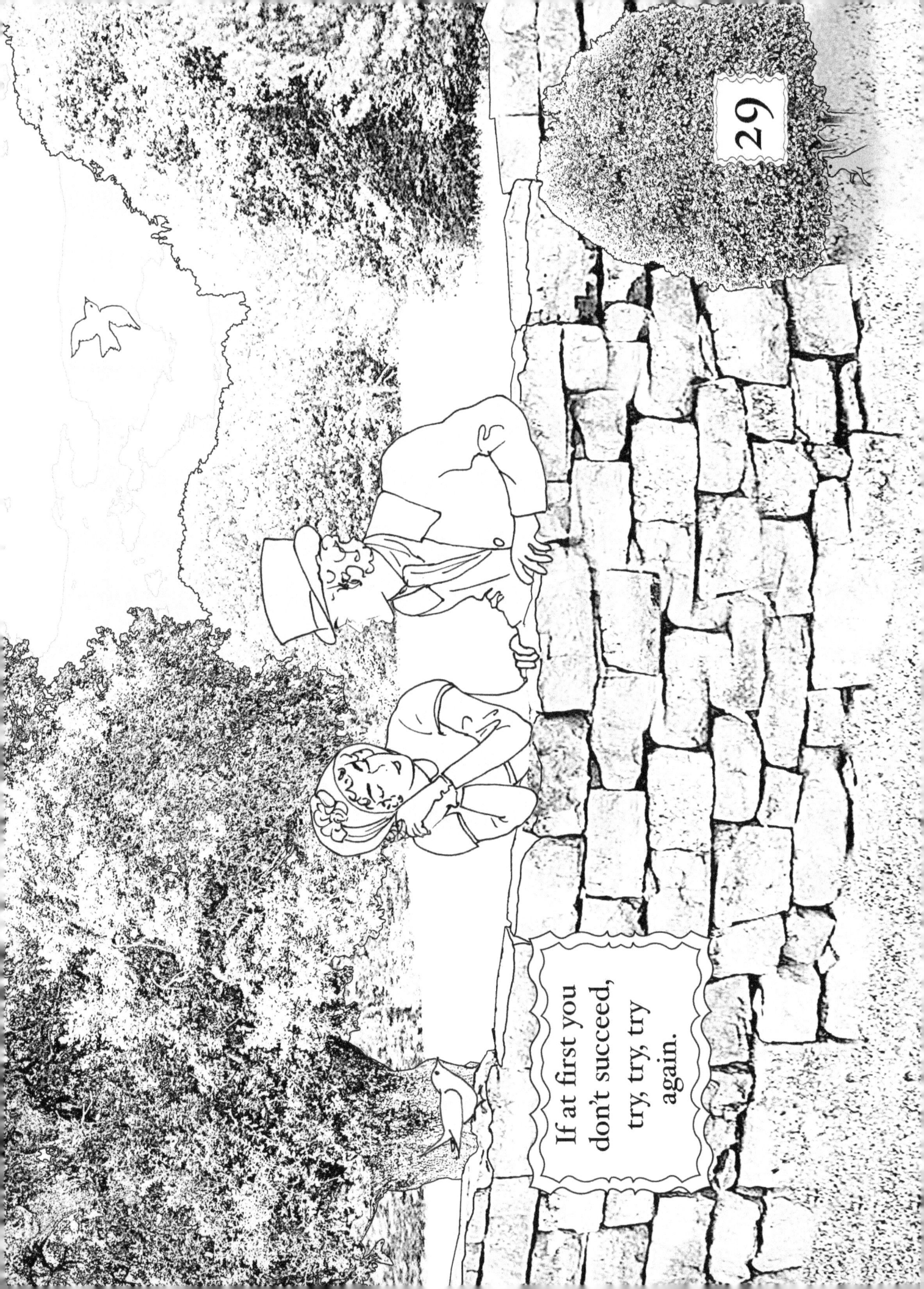

If at first you don't succeed, try, try, try again.

29

This would be a great place for a dazzling sunset. What little sky you have above the house, you have much more reflected in the pond below it. Go ahead and make it a colorer's grand finale.

Make sure to sign it on the cover!

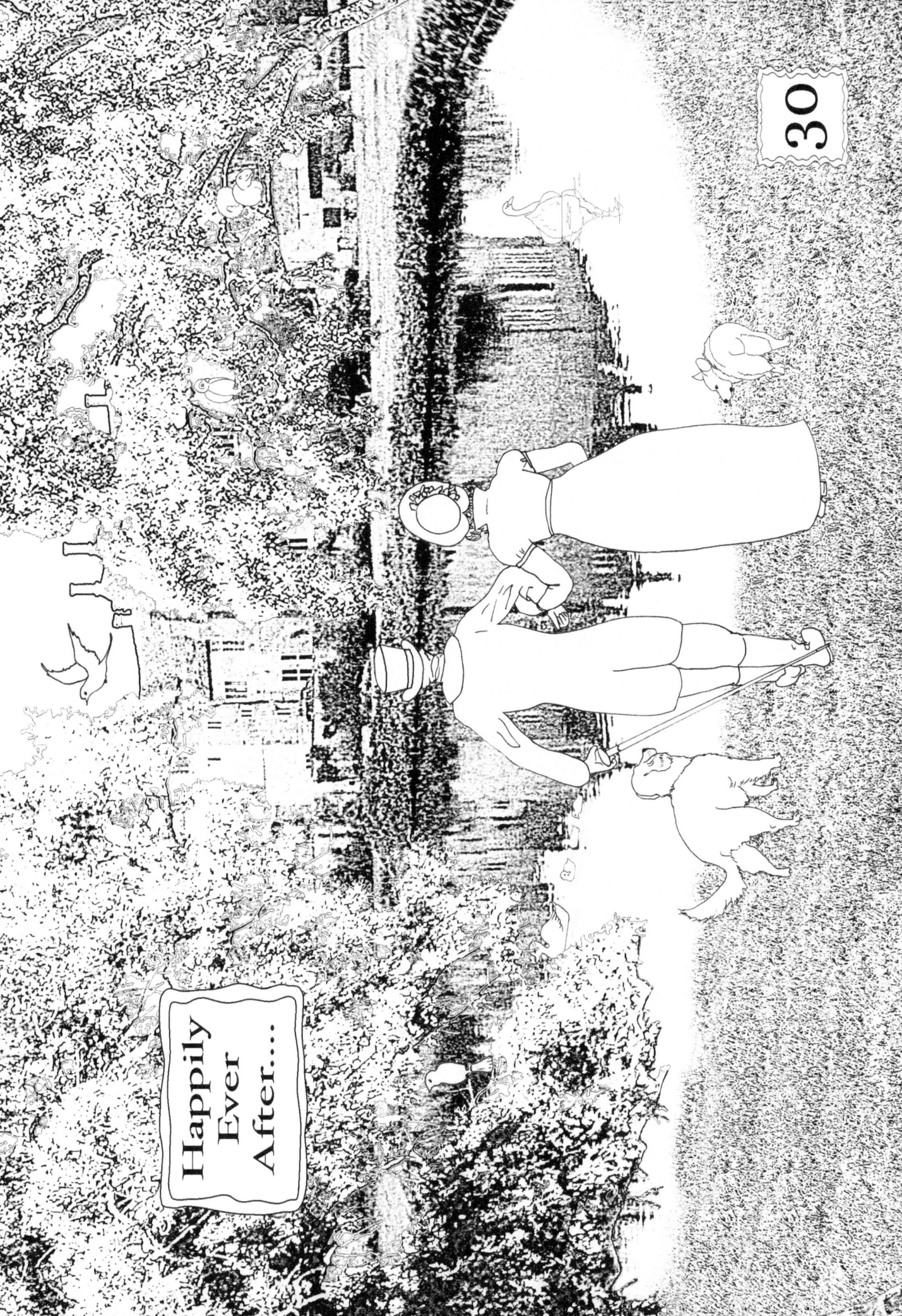

Happily
Ever
After....

30

www.ingramcontent.com/pod-product-compliance
Lightning Source LLC
Chambersburg PA
CBHW080630190526
45169CB00009B/3348